LETTERS *to* MICKEY

BY THE FRIENDS & FANS OF MICKEY MANTLE

HarperCollins*Publishers*

Mickey C. Mantle conceived the idea for this book. The Mickey Mantle Foundation and MultiCom Partners Ltd. developed the concept on behalf of The Mickey Mantle Foundation. Special thanks to Alyssa, Ashley, and Andrea True for their volunteer work.

Jim Borgman cartoon reprinted with special permission of King Features Syndicate.
Bob Englehart cartoon reprinted with special permission of the artist and The Hartford Courant.
"St. Peter" cartoon reprinted with special permission of Bob Deore, Dallas Morning News, and Universal Press Syndicate.

Memorabilia photographs copyright © 1995 by Cathy Camarata. Used by permission.

HarperCollins books may be purchased for educational, business, or sales promotional use. For information please write: Special Markets Department, HarperCollins Publishers, Inc., 10 East 53rd Street, New York, NY 10022.

FIRST EDITION

Designed by Caitlin Daniels

ISBN 0-06-018362-4

95 96 97 98 99 RRD 10 9 8 7 6 5 4 3 2 1

LETTERS *to* MICKEY

Mickey C. Mantle
Dallas, Texas

August 9, 1995

Dear Friends and Fans:

During my eighteen years as a New York Yankee I felt blessed that I could play baseball, a game I love so much. God gave me the strength, talent and courage to play the game the way I felt it should be played. But it was my teammates that gave me the support and friendship I needed to find my place among great players, coaches and managers. Until I entered the Betty Ford Clinic in January of 1994 to overcome my problem with alcohol, and, then underwent my liver transplant in June of 1995 at Baylor University Medical Center, I did not think that I would ever experience that kind of support and friendship again. I was wrong.

I entered the Betty Ford Clinic embarrassed and regretful that I had let alcohol abuse effect my life, my family and my career. Those regrets continue, but because of you, your letters, cards and prayers I once again felt an overwhelming rush of support and friendship. And then my liver transplant occurred. I was given a second chance by that gift of life. Once more you were there with thousands of letters and cards expressing your support and friendship. Again, I was overwhelmed.

I think God must have wanted me to be an example to people and to do something important with this extra time. I believe I need to speak out about the danger of alcohol. I believe I need to speak out about the need for everyone to become an organ donor so that life can go on for others as a result of one's death. I also believe, God wanted me to have this opportunity to answer your thousands of cards and letters that meant so much to me and my family.

I caused to be formed The Mickey Mantle Foundation which will be dedicated to fund an endowment for a chair for transplant research at Baylor University Medical Center and to form "Mickey's Team" an organ donor educational and awareness effort to make organ donation a universally accepted act of kindness in which we can each find comfort at the time of our death or that of our loved ones. I am hoping that companies, large and small, and people, rich and poor, will join my team.

With this letter to you many friends and fans that gave me the support and friendship I needed, I want to say that it meant the world to me. I have, with the help of my family, selected some of the letters and cards you sent me so that I can share them with the world. I wish I could have published all of them - they were all important. This book is to be published and sold and all of the royalties are to be paid into The Mickey Mantle Foundation to benefit those we can help. This would not have been possible had each of you not taken the time to write me your thoughts and shared your feelings. You didn't know it at the time, but you became part of "Mickey's Team". The love you gave me will now be shared with others. You were my teammates in my most difficult times. You picked me up and helped me continue. You kept me in the game when I had my doubts. For that, and all the support I enjoyed during my years as an active player, I say "Thank You" from the bottom of my heart. Thanks for being there.....

Your Teammate

Mickey

"GO HIT ME ONE MORE HOME RUN, MICK....."

Dear Mickey,

When I heard that you were sick, my mind went back to a day when I was a kid. I was watching a Yankee game on TV, and you came up to bat all taped up as usual. You proceeded to hit a left handed home run off the facade in right field in old Yankee stadium. As you hobbled around the bases I realized that tears were streaming down my face. I had just seen my hero do the impossible. I'm now a grown man and you're still my hero. You always will be.

Get well soon.

Sincerely

Bob Leittan

Peck Owens Company

Mickey Mantle
Baylor Univ. Hosp.
Dallas TX 75246

Dear Mick,

About some 40 + years ago I sold you what was
probably your 1st good ball glove; A Marty Marion
G-600 for around $9.00 and you paid it out in 3
payments of $3.00 @..

We at Owens Sporting Goods were rooting hard for
you to make it then, and you did!!

And We are rooting even harder for you to make it
now, AND YOU WILL!!

Just hang in there & keep fighting!

Our very best to you
Sincerely,

Peck Owens

Peck Owens

Formerly- Owens Sporting Goods,
Joplin, MO.

PS, I'm not sure whether you were playing for the
Whiz Kids, Barney Barnett, or the Joplin Miners..
Its been too long ago.

9 August 1995

Dear Mickey,

Fight the good fight, dear friend. And most of all, forgive yourself.
You gave millions of us so much happiness. Everytime the Yankees came
to Memorial Stadium to play the Orioles, we (my husband and I and three
little boys) were there. What wonderful fun that was. My sons are
all grown up now, married with families, and I have been a widow for
20 years. But I think back often on those joyful times.

I must tell you a little story; one night, after the game, my youngest
son, about 6 or 7 years old at the time, grew very quiet as we drove
home. I looked in the back seat, and there he sat with an older
brother on each side of him. I asked him if he was O. K. And his
reply - "Mom, were you ever that close to Mickey Mantle before?" He
was on the proverbial cloud nine - absolutely mesmerized by your
game performance that evening. I don't remember which team won that
game - but I'll bet the Yankees did. That little boy and his older
brothers began playing Little League ball as soon as they were able,
and all three played Pony League games. We are truly a baseball
family. And, Yes - we have season tickets to the Orioles' games
at Camden Yards. We are avid Cal Ripken fans and are awaiting the
big day when he breaks Lou Gehrig's consecutive games record.

God bless you, Mickey. This old world is a better place for your
having lived in it. My family and I are praying for your complete
recovery.

By the way, we have three recovering alcholics in our extended family -
doesn't every family have at least one? It takes lots of courage,
and you again have set the example for many of us.

With love and prayers,

Joyce Lundmark
(For the Lundmark family)

PS We will also remember your wife and boys in our prayers.

Dear Mick.

I'm a 49 year old who grew up worshipping the GREAT MICKEY MANTLE when I was a young boy who lived, ate and drank NY Yankee baseball as a young boy and have found out that not much has changed through the years.

You did it all and you did it soooooooo good! Mick, I'm married, the father of two, a Vietnam Vet (66-67) and work on the local police department and feel I've been around a corner or two but like so many others I know, just get goose bumps when the name Mickey Mantle is mentioned. I've read all your books and many others - hell, I probably know more about you than you do!!!! But what a thrill it is was for me to see my daughter, a pitcher on her high school fast pitch team put on her uniform with the good old # 7 (she had first pick of any number) !

You need to get better - fast. Not for you so much, but for thousands like me who can live with assassinations, Vietnam, and bombings, but can't stand the thought of losing THE MICK. Please, get better quickly. Hell, I'd give you my own liver - you gave us your heart!

You were, and ARE - the greatest, my friend.

Thanks for the Memories,

Richard Good

Richard G. Good, Sr.

MR. MANTLE,

I AM NOT MUCH OF A LETTER WRITER. IN fact, this is the first time I have ever done this. THERE ARE many things I would like you to know. However, I am going to keep this brief. As a boy growing up in the "fifties" you were my hero. My feelings toward Mickey Mantle were more than idolizing a baseball player. You made my life more exciting, more pleasant, more rewarding, and a thousand other adjectives too numerous to mention. THESE feelings have not dimmed over the years. I want to thank you for making a young mans' life much more worthwhile then it otherwise would have been.

I want you to know my son, Mickey Charles Mantle Lippy, and I are praying for your speedy recovery every night.

WITH DEEP RESPECT AND ADMIRATION,
Bruce Lippy

Dear Mr. Mantle,

My name is Alisha Killion
I heard you had a liver transplant.
On February 10, 1994 I had a heart transplant
I am ten years old now, but was eight at the
time. You may feel the recovery is long,
but it may go quicker than you think.
By the next May I was ready to strat
school with my class.

I heard that you are looking forward to
playing golf. I like most all sports, but
my best sport is basketball. Here is a
picture of me when I played at our
YMCA. We only lost one game. My
favorite position is point guard. I hope
to try out for our school team next
year.

Now I am enjoying all kinds of things
and I hope you soon will be too!

Sincerely, Alisha Killion

August 15, 1995

Mrs. Mickey Mantle
The Mickey Mantle Foundation
8080 North Central Expressway
Dallas, Texas 75206

Dear Mrs. Mantle:

Hillary and I were sorry to learn of your husband's death.

Mickey's talent on the baseball diamond, his grace, speed, and tape-measure power, thrilled baseball fans of all ages, serving as an inspiration to so many. He was a legendary part of baseball's royal tradition -- a Yankee and a winner -- and generations will long cherish the memories he left.

I know his last days were not easy, but Hillary and I admired his efforts to get a message to America's youngsters, however painful it was for him.

We hope that you will find comfort in the loving support of your family and friends. You are in our thoughts and prayers.

Sincerely,

Bill Clinton

Dear Mr. Mantle,

My name is Nathan Price and my little brother Patricks. I'm sorry your not feeling well. But this might cheer you up. My dad is sick alot also he says you were the best baseball player in the world. He also said you had a prison, whatever that is, about the game. We used to play baseball alot but now he's to tired and sick. The docter told him when he gets a new liver he will be going again, can they really do that? My mom got sick and died 3 years ago. I didn't tell anyone, but I'm scared that my dad may not come back from the hospial. I know he's scared to, sometimes he just sits at the desk and looks at papers. I hear him on the telephone talking and crying about not having enough money to pay bills and not having a place to live. It hurts me to see my dad like this. Can you write back to tell me how you paid your bills and stuff. If I could know How, then I could suprize my dad with enough money and He wouldn't cry and worry so much. Plese call or write real soon. My dad's name is Joey.
                    Thanks for Reading this,
Aug 9, 1995   Nathan Price

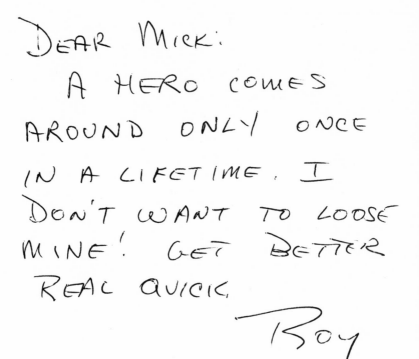

Dear Mick:
   A HERO COMES
AROUND ONLY ONCE
IN A LIFETIME. I
DON'T WANT TO LOOSE
MINE! GET BETTER
REAL QUICK.
                    Roy

February 16, 1994

Hello Mickey,

From Worcester, Ma — admiration and best wishes!
Ever since I caught a long foul ball from your bat in Fenway
Park in 1958, I've followed your exploits with daily interest.
By the way, the ball is signed by Ted Williams while he was in
the New England Baptist Hospital after crashing into the Green
Monster. My daughter was a nurse on his floor.

Perhaps the chief reason I'm writing is that I remember
the few years alcohol got the better of me and my pastoral
ministry was interrupted while I got help. Since 1976 I've
been sober and am very grateful for those who helped me and
encouraged me to believe life is worth living.

I think of you often and trust that all will be O.K.
I know that you can't live on memories, but memories do
provide an amazing amount of great feelings. I played
semi-pro baseball in the 50's & 60's in Maine while I preached
in the Auburn area. Occasionally I can recall a special
moment in a playoff game and actually feel the past.
You've a great many of such—and many more good times
ahead.

Strange - I've caught two balls at Fenway - and both off
your bat. They are my favorite baseball items.

warmly,
Paul Ferrin

6-8-95

Mick:

Please get well
soon. We I need you

Dear Mickey,

I saw your interview last night on <u>NOW</u> with Bob Costas and I felt I had to write to you.

I was one of those kids growing up in the 60's who Bob Costas referred to as having you as a role model / hero. I followed your career since I can remember, read everything I could find about you and watched you on TV and movies. Growing up in Massachusetts in the middle of Red Sox territory it was not the most popular thing to be a Yankee fan. I loved every minute of it! I did try to emulate you as an athlete and that probably is a part of why I went into physical education / coaching

You were on a pedastal when I was a kid; not realizing that you were human too. When I first heard of your drinking problem I had many emotions, even at 38 years of age you still are a "hero" to me. After listening to you I have even more respect for you. The same traits you showed as an athlete - strength, courage, tenacity - seem to work for you in your present battles. I hope I can be as strong when tradgety strikes me as it surely will some time in my life.

You still are a hero to me but for more deeper reasons than "your just a ballplayer"; you are a great human being and I admire your courage and pray you win this battle and get closer to your sons.

Thank you for such fantastic memories and bestof luck to you in your future.

Sincerely,
Bill Kaste

8/11/95

Dear Mickey —

I'm sure you know, along with life's wonders are life's tragedies. I'm finding myself having to endure the passing of my heroes, my loved ones + friends alike. A guy like me rarely gets an opportunity to even meet my heroes let alone develop a relationship with them. But, there's no mistaking the degree of pain when someone you don't even know is going through peril... You love them just the same as those you know real well. Now one of my biggest heroes is ailing and my pain is not diminished as are my prayers, heartfelt and sincere. Mickey, you have already given me everything you could and you don't even know it. Well, now you do. I'm nobody to you and naturally, at a time like this, you want to spend every precious moment with your friends and family.

For whatever its worth, Mick, you are forever in my heart and I wish you the best...

Thanks for the thrills.

Your fan,

David Bernstein

January 31, 1994

Mr. Mickey Mantle
c/o The Betty Ford Center
Eisenhower Medical Center
39000 Bob Hope Drive
El Rancho Mirage, California 92064

Dear Mr. Mantle,

It was with great sadness that I read about your life-long struggle against alcohol, and about the terrible problems that it has caused you. I wish you great strength and unfailing determination as you now enter your rehabilitation program at the Betty Ford Center. I sincerely believe that the same earnest tenacity of purpose that characterized your baseball years will successfully see you through this transitional period, and bring you to a new life, free from your former illness. Please accept my every best wish for a full recovery.

Although you would never remember our meeting over 30 years ago, I was a regular at Yankee Stadium during the early 1960's. My friends and I, all children, would buy cheap, upper-deck seats, and then sneak down into the seats behind the right fielder in the late innings. This happened with such frequency one particular season that Roger Maris came to know us by our first names. One day, you were passing through right field and spoke with us for a moment. It was a tremendous thrill, one that I will never forget. You were then, and still are, one of baseball's greatest legends. I consider it a great honor that I had the opportunity to watch you play.

Again, please accept my best wishes for a complete recovery, with many years of health and happiness to follow!

Sincerely,

March 30, 1994

Mr. Mickey Mantle
Care of Bob Costas
NBC TV
30 Rockefeller Plaza
N.Y. N.Y. 10112

Dear Mr. Mantle:

After watching your interview with Bob Costas this evening, I wanted to write and share my thoughts with you.

As a boy growing up in the mountains of western North Carolina, baseball was an important part of my everyday life. My childhood memories are filled with countless sandlot games, trading bubble gum cards, playing catch with Dad and following your games in the box scores. I think the first book I ever read was Mickey Mantle's "Profiles of Courage". This book contained a collection of short stories about athletes overcoming obstacles and personal tragedies.

My grandfather once gave me a ball with your autograph on it. At that time I was about 8 years old. Well, like most boys I was always in need of a baseball....and I remember one day I had to choose between keeping that ball as it was or using it for a ballgame. Naturally, I thought what would Mickey do? Of course ... I chose to play ball. You can imagine my grandfather's dismay when he found out that your autograph was smacked right off that ball. No regrets, I only did what any self-respecting ballplayer would do.

I'm now 38 years old and still consider myself a "Mickey Mantle fan". Not only do I admire your accomplishments as the greatest switch hitter the game has ever known but more importantly I admire your courage to confront your alcoholism at the Betty Ford clinic. I wish you and your family the best.

Thank you for being Mickey Mantle... a profile of courage.

Sincerely,

Jack H. Rogers, III

16

Mickey Mantle
c/o Betty Ford Center
Rancho Mirage, California

Thirty five years ago, as a small child, I admired your baseball skills. I still think of you as the greatest player the game will ever see.

I read today that you entered the Betty Ford Center. I am not sad to read this. I am pleased that my childhood baseball idol is an even bigger man than I dreamed.

I respect the courage you have shown in your recent decision. I wish you a rapid and complete recovery

Tom Temple

August 1, 1995

Dear Mr. Mantle,

I am sorry to hear that you are back in the hospital. I
have a true little story about you that I think you might enjoy
reading.

In 1972 when my son Scott was only 6, we boarded an airplane
on our way to Disney World. Scott was quite filled with
anticipation at all the things he would be seeing and doing. To
add to this excitement, my husband saw you seated in the airplane
a few rows behind us. He whipped out a pen and slip of paper and
told Scott that Mickey Mantle was back there and you might give
him an autograph. In a few minutes my son returned with a
strange and slightly dejected look on his face. I said, "What's
wrong, honey? Wouldn't Mickey Mantle give you his autograph?"
"Yes," he said. "But I thought you said Mickey Mouse!"

Please do not feel slighted by this anecdote. Scott is now
totally aware of who you are and is greatly distressed by your
illness as are we all. We pray that our gracious Lord will grant
you full recovery and extend to you a long and happy life.

Sincerely,

Nita Bertram

Nita Bertram

10 Aug 95

Mickey,

There's one thing cancer can't take from you — your millions of fans who will always remember you.

God bless you my friend and thanks for the memories.

Jim Tunney

Dear Mickey –

I am a 72 year old grandmother whose children and grandchildren know you are the best thing that ever happened to baseball and their lives. They had and still have an honest-to-God real person who they have always looked up to. My oldest son, Ernie, is now 45. He can still talk about your hey-days, RBI's, S.O.S, and the distance your home runs went. If his dad hadn't walked out and left us I know Ernie could have been something in pro ball. When his dad left, Ernie's heart went with him. My daughter, Mary Ellen always thought you were "cute". You know girls. My youngest boy, Michael, never got too far in baseball but Ernie had done his job on Michael also about you. To this day Mickey they feel about you the same as when you were their high-light of baseball. Now I have a Grand-son, Grant, 8 yrs. old and ready to take on the little leagues this spring. He asked for and got a plaque with your picture on it plus a Mickey Mantle comic book. He can also quote your stats. I stood in line down in Washington, D.C. with my grand daughter to get your autograph on your book for Ernie. He was really upset that he couldn't go but it was a break for me and my grand daughter.

I want you to know how this one family loves you for what you brought to all of us. We're proud of you for taking on this latest project with the Betty Ford Foundation. We know you again will come out on top. Our prayers and wishes are with you always.

Sincerely,

Margaret Boswell

Dear Mickey

   On my desk at the office is a photograph of me taken
with you at Civic Stadium in the seventies. This photo is
the pride of my collection of baseball heroes. Yes,
Mickey you are my hero. You have been my greatest hero
since early childhood.

   I coach little league baseball because of you, my love
for the game was formulated while watching Whitey Ford and
Roger Maris work their magic on the field. I developed my
future philosophy of life watching you stretch a single
into a double. I first understood the possibilities of
achievement when I'd read about your courage in the face
of pain and injuries. Never let it be said that you
didn't give your best effort, even under the influence you
shone above the rest.

   A client, after seeing the photo, asked to shake my
hand the other day. Surprised I offer my hand, he said "
I just want to be able to say that I shook the hand of a
man who shook the hand of Mickey Mantle." We spent the
next few minutes remembering #7 and the many great
memories we shared from those great Yankee years. I pray
for a speedy recovery and better days ahead for you. God
bless you.

Hal

Hal Andrews

Dear Mickey,

I have been a big fan of yours and the yankees since I was growing up in Indiana and later after moving to New York. I wish you a full and speedy recovery.

My husband died suddenly on 6/7/95 and I made a decision to donate his organs. Learning of your transplant the following morning only reassured me that I had made the right decision. I hope your story will encourage others to do the same.

While you may not have received my husband's liver, I will always feel a special closeness to you because of the coincidence of the two events.

All good wishes for the future to you and your family,

Sincerely,
Susan Thompson

23

"The Kid In Me"

An All American crew cut kid
With an Oklahoma drawl
Came to play in '52
The game of Big League ball.
He played in Yankee pinstripes
And he batted left or right
And he could make the pitcher sweat
Before the ball took flight
Toward hands and arms hard as steel
And a body like coiled spring,
Through eagle eyes he'd see the pitch
Then loose his mighty swing
And hit the ball like cannonfire
Way back into the stands....
Then 'round the bases he would trot
To applause from all his fans.
I dreamed he felt a shiver
When he first walked hallowed sod
While ghosts of all great players passed
Looked on and gave their nod
For him to play where they had played
And had made the people cheer....
From time to time I'm sure they whispered
In the youthful player's ear,
"Play your best with all your heart
 And always love the game
 So fans can one day see you
 In the cherished Hall of Fame
 And little boys grown into men
 Can one day tell their sons
 All about the crew cut kid
 And all the things he's done."

Half a mile or more I'd walk
To a little country store
With the nickle I had earned
By doing all my chores
And buy a pack of baseball cards
Then sit down on a crate,
Just hoping I would find his picture
There posing at the plate.
Such golden days to be a boy
Or a shining baseball star,
Just to know that in my dreams
I could hit a ball so far
And glide across the outfield green
With graceful speed so fleet
Or safely slide in a dusty cloud
And bring them cheering to their feet
Or throw the ball from centerfield
And bounce it off homeplate
To come to rest in Yogi's mitt
And seal the runner's fate.
Oh Glory, what Glory to be a boy
Dreaming all these thoughts
Of facing nine men on the field
In battles won and fought.
If not for him I wouldn't have
These dreams of mine at all,
That All American crew cut kid
With an Oklahoma drawl.

Jim Loring

8-4-95

Dear Mickey,

I am sorry to learn of your illness but admire your courage and determination in handling it.

As a boy, I was a Dodger fan and therefore carried a grudge against the Yankees because you always beat the Dodgers, or so it seemed. But as the years passed, I came to appreciate the

greatness of the Yankees —
and you — and now realize
how truly great you were.
Like most of the population,
I revere you and your
Yankees.

I'm presently reading "My
Favorite Summer" and like it.
It brings back lots of memories

I'm talking to a friend
about you yesterday, he asked —
who will our next hero be?"
neither of us knew the answer.
I wish you the best.

MORGAN METCALF

Dear Mr. Mantle,

I know you receive hundreds of letters everyday wishing you well, but ever since your recent surgery, I have wanted to write and tell you this story. I hope it will make you smile.

When I was growing up during the early to mid sixties, with my brother & sister, my parents would take us to visit my Great Grandmother in NE Iowa. She was an avid fan of yours. So much to the <u>point</u>, that if you and your Yankees were playing and we came to visit, she would say hello & not speak to us kids until the game was over. Many times we would go outside to play and she would lock us out of her house so we wouldn't disrupt her watching Mickey Mantle. She loved us very much, but when you were playing - you came first!

My Great Grandmother passed away in 1972 at the ripe age of 98. The fondest memory that I have of her was her admiration of a baseball player named Mickey Mantle.

Thank you Mr. Mantle for making my Great Grandmothers life a little richer and thank you for the memory I have of her and you. I hope that your treatments and recovery will all go well. I will keep you and your family in my prayers. God grant you all the Strength and courage that you need for a speedy and full recovery -

Sincerely
Connie E. Whan

Dear Mickey:

One of the things, when a child is growing up, that he looks up to is his real life heroes, those people he would most like to pattern themselves after. Living in Montreal Canada during the 50's and 60's, I was of course a Montreal Canadiens hockey fan and the players who I emulated the most were Maurice Richard and Doug Harvey. My parents however, went on a vacation in 1953 to New York and they brought me back a New York Yankees baseball cap. I was, from that day forward, the most devout Yankees fan in my school and neighbourhood, and often the only one, and there was one person above all the others who was my immediate hero, Mickey Charles Mantle.

Every young lad should have a real life hero to look up to, and maybe you don't really realize it, but you have single-handedly guided countless young people in life through your athletic prowess, but just as importantly, though your grit and determination. In my last year of baseball, when I was mired in a batting slump and hitting just .111 and wanted to quit, my dad asked me if I thought that " Mickey " would just quit. Well, I want to tell you that I ended the season with a .591 average and an even greater respect for life and how to handle problems. So, you see, you are a great person to countless people whom you don't even know. No person is perfect, we all have flaws and we are all faced with tragedy, but it is how we face it that really counts. I know, because I too have lost a son, and in my case, my only son. But I have a wonderful little 11 year old daughter, and she has taken up baseball this summer, and I can assure you she sure will know all about the great Mickey Mantle. Yesaterday, she asked me if there really was a Babe Ruth, and I said " yes Angela, but there is someone who was even greater, and his name is Mickey Mantle, and he is having some problems right now, but he will overcome them. " So, you see Mick, you are touching another generation, and even girl's lives. You may be the biological father of three boys, but you are the guiding influence to many more, and I would like you to know that you were a part of my up-bringing, and I thank you for that, because I didn't turn out too bad.

IT IS NOT ALWAYS IMPORTANT WHAT YOU DID WITH PARTS OF YOUR PAST AS IT IS WITH WHAT YOU DO WITH THE REST OF YOUR LIFE !!.

God bless you !! and Thank you for all the wonderful memories and for all that you mean to so many people who are praying for you and wishing you the very best ! A person's existance may be judged by the way that they have affected in a positive manner the many lives of those they have come in contact with, both directly and indirectly, and if that is the case, then you are a darn good person, and a great DAMN YANKEE.

Looking forward to seeing that infectous smile of yours again, and maybe some day I will be lucky enough to meet you personally and to THANK YOU personally for all you have meant to me.

Robert (Bob) Barnett

A Lifelong Mickey Mantle Fan

Miami June 6, 1995

Mr. Mickey Mantle
Baylor University Medical Center
Dallas, Texas

Dear Mickey:
Today while reading the Sport pages of the Miami Herald, I came across of the very sad news of you current health condition.

I do not know why, but like magic it came into my mind, for few minutes I was transported back to Yankee Stadium the day of your retirement.

Back then I was a kid living in New York, my parents did not have a lot of money, but I had to be there with you on that day, I knew that my Father could not get us tickets, but I had to be there with you on that day.

The solution was to take an extra paper (The Long Island Star Journal) route to make the extra money, I did Exactly that, because I had to be there with you on that day.

As a kid I never had a day like that day, I was happy because I was there with you on that day, yet I remember crying my heart out, because after that day, MY HERO, WILL NEVER PLAY AGAIN.

As yesterday, today I am there with you, as yesterday I am happy because some how, I am getting in touch with the only HERO I ever had, as yesterday, today my eyes are filled with tears for you.

There is not much that I can do for you, but I promise you, that you will be in my daily prayers, also I am enclosing a small card that y have carried in my wallet for a long time, please read it and keep it close to you.

Keep the Faith, you may be thinking that this may be the bottom of the ninth, with two outs, trailing by one run; Take a second look, there is a <u>MAN</u> on first and **MICKEY MANTLE AT BAT.**

May God Bless you,

Hector H. Romero.

THIS ONE'S FOR YOU, MICKEY!

You came out of Oklahoma
To fulfill your childhood dream
To play the game of baseball
For the New York Yankees team

It wasn't long before we knew
That all had not been told
As the quiet boy from Oklahoma
You were worth your weight in gold

You could hit the ball from either side
And knock it out of the park
You did it more than 500 times
Until your legs began to fall apart

You won the triple crown
And took it all in fun
You weren't one to boast or brag
About what you had done

I had hoped to meet you one day
But I was simply just too late
For your body began to give way
To what soon would be your fate

You refused to leave without a fight
And made us all aware
Of the need to be a donor
To show others how much we care

Once again you were a hero
You showed us the importance of giving
Many people signed the cards to help
So others have a chance at living

You passed away this summer
And went to your place of rest
I know that few will disagree
I think you were the very best

I hope they're playing baseball
When you walk through the heavenly gate.
I can just hear the roar of the crowd
When number 7 steps up to the plate.

And as I step to the plate, I think of you!
When from my family I hear
"Let's go Mickey" I feel very proud
Of the nickname I hold so dear.

I love to play centerfield like you.
The number seven I proudly wear
I like to bat with the bases full
For the pitchers I have no fear.

Then I hear the hum of the pitch
And the crack of my bat rings true.
As I round the bases I look up to the sky
And think .... "Thanks Mickey, this one's for you!"

Casey Cox, (#7), Age 13

Jan. 31, 1994

Dear Mickey,

I read in my home town newspaper this morning that you're at the Betty Ford Center for treatment of alcohol abuse. My feelings and emotions were strong and mixed. I feel badly that you must face and deal with this difficult problem, but on the other hand I'm very glad that you're getting the help you need.

Alcohol touches most of our lives in this country, and it's usually not very pretty. I'm very familiar with the difficult struggles you're now facing. I want you to know that I support your efforts and courage. You've made the most difficult and important decision of all... admitting that you do have a problem and doing something about it.

As a youngster growing up you personified for me the qualities of courage, perseverence, athletic ability and a winning attitude which help me to personally deal with my own life and problems. Now you must once again call upon these traits and many more to help you fight your most difficult battle. I guess as the years passed I suspected you might have a problem, but I too chose to deny it.

Rather than ramble on and get into a lot of "fan" stuff, I'm simply going to close, because some how it seems like neither the time nor the place. However, it is the time and place to encourage you and assure you that I'm with you all the way and I shall be praying for you.

We've met once before, but I sincerely hope we shall meet again. I'd love to buy you . . . a cup of coffee.

Sincerely,
Dr. Ed Kampf

Dear Mr. Mantle,
As a kid you have
always been my
baseball hero, and
you still are. I am
legally blind, but
enjoyed watching you.
You were like a big
brother for, & to me,
so I wish you the
very best. Get
well quick.

your friends
and avid
fan,
. Bruce

Hi Mickey,

I'm one of the silent _majority_ in America that think you are great! I'm 47 years old. Although we've never met, I feel that I know you very well. I've even read all your books.

I've always loved Baseball. From my earliest memories, I recall rushing home from school for lunch where Mom would have lunch ready and the TV on the World Series. I cherished every moment that I could watch my favorite team, the New York Yankees, and my favorite player, Mickey Mantle. Although I knew all the Yankees, you were my hero! To this day, I remember your distinctive mannerisms; the way you jogged the bases when you hit one out, the way you swung the bat, the way you chased a fly ball in centerfield.

I most remember the way you carried yourself when you hit one out or made a great catch; No high fives, no wild emotion. Cool and calm. It was as though you expected to succeed. I wanted to be just like you.

I'm sorry that I haven't written to you long before now. I know you've had some tough times, especially lately.

I want you to know you're in my prayers and I love ya, Mick! You'll always be my hero!

Sincerely,
George Faulkner

Dear Mickey,

Please get well soon.
We are praying for
you.
We love you!
Your a very good
baseball player.
Sincerly
Tiffany Mercer

Dear Mr. Mantle,

I send you my wishes for a speedy recovery,
and a new life as you begin to feel stronger
and stronger.

I can't say enough about how you made my
childhood something special. As a young woman
shut out by the "little league world" in the 1960's,
my only salvation, my only way to escape from
a world and a home where my father drank was
to watch you and the Yankees on television, and the
occasional thrilling trip to the Stadium. I can not tell
you how special you are and always will be to me.

I admired you when you struggled with your legs,
watching your transition from the outfield to the
infield during those years. I collected your trading
cards with the littleboys in my class, always looking
for a Mickey.

Today as a doctor, I have tremendous compassion
and understanding about what you are presently
undergoing. I offer you my prayers and my daily
thoughts for your recovery.

Mr. Mantle, you are our treasure, and I wanted to
write this letter for 30 years now, and finally I am
doing it. Thank you for hanging in there for me to
get this opportunity. Thank you for getting sober,
thank you for passing that sobriety to your your boys,
and thank you for helping me dream through a childhood
that at times was very hard.

With admiration, and love,

Dr. Joan Fallon

June 8, 1995

Mickey Mantle
Baylor University Medical Center
3500 Gaston Avenue
Dallas, Texas 75246

Dear Mickey:

In 1966 you did a wonderful deed for me and my family. I do not expect that you remember the occasion. I was so taken back by your kindness and understanding that I do not even remember telling you "thank you" but your generosity has never been forgotten.

My family and I were new to Dallas...My husband having just left the Navy and starting a new job with Braniff Airways. We met you in a small private club on Lovers Lane called "The Town Pump" (the pilots hangout) and if my memory does not fail me you were a neighbor to Jim Barrigan, the owner.

Braniff paid very little to new pilots and with 2 children of our own, a car payment, rent, etc., I was extremely concerned about not having enough money to buy christmas presents for our nieces and nephews and had too much pride to admit it to our families. During a conversation with some of my friends at the club explaining my plight, you sent me to the "dime store" next door to buy baseballs and took the time to personally autograph all of them. Our nieces and nephews had a christmas present that year beyond comparison.

Mickey, you have had a special place in my heart all of these years and I have been remiss in telling you. Thank you, you are a very special person.

I pray everyday for your speedy recovery.

May God bless you,

Judy Ford

MICKEY MANTLE
BAYLOR MEDICAL CENTER
35 GASTON AVE
DALLAS TX 75246

MICK:
I'VE BEEN FOLLOWING YOUR PROGRESS AND AM HAPPY THINGS ARE GOING IN
THE RIGHT DIRECTION FOR YOU.   KEEP IT GOING.   GOOD LUCK.

    SINCERELY ARNOLD PALMER

Dear Mickey,

I grew up in Blackwell, Oklahoma, early 60s, playing a sincere but iffy right field in the "pee-wee" league. Our team called themselves The Newland Window and Storm Door Co. Bluejays.

Those days, even way out there on the prairie, amid the corn fields, the wheat... the way my teammates and I judged it, no baseball team on God's green earth even came close to touching the almighty New York Yankees.

We ranked you guys ("you guys" being mostly you: Mickey Mantle, and of course, that other legend, Roger Maris) right up there with the early American astronauts, the Mercury bunch -- incontestable heroes like Alan Shepard, John Glenn, Gordon Cooper.

In fact, in our flabbergasted retellings of you guys' exploits, we often described the spectacular flies you slammed as bouncing off Mercury capsules in space!

Those were my 1960s, my generation.

One year my Grampa Newland got up some nerve and a lotta dough and took not only our team, but the whole grungy, stinky crewcut pee-wee league up to Kansas City, for us to witness you guys, live and for real and in person, beat the living tar outta the Kansas City Athletics.

There in the rich green grass, the brown white-striped baselines, in all your brash young glory...

There were YOU GUYS... Mantle and Maris (God rest him).

I'll never _ever_ forget that day as long as I live.

It lives, _it lives as part of me._

Seeing the stuff on TV now, about the shape you were in, your transplant, and how it appears to be going better, I cannot help but think back to that afternoon in Kansas City when I was just a kid, and you were one of the finest sluggers ever.

Thank you for a lasting memory. I <u>do</u> hope you get better soon. One of your many fans, wishing you the best,

Mike Newland

Dear Mickey — 6/95
Your humility and
courage have always
made you a hero.
I am a better man
today for the things I
saw in you long ago.
—Peter Laskowich

Dear Mr. Mantle,

My name is Karen Lombardo. I am 8 years old.
This is the fourth letter I've sent
you. I don't know if you're gotten any,
but I'm going to keep trying. I hope
you feel better. I've been listening to
the news to see how you are feeling.
I've been keeping you in my prayers.

You are my favorite player!
I bet I am your biggest fan!
I learned all about you from my dad.
My Dad told me how great you were.
He also told me that you have
had some rough times in your
life. I want you to know that I don't
care about that. You are still my hero.
This summer Mom & Dad are
taking me to Cooperstown.

My mom said she would take my picture
in front of your plaque. I'll try
to send you a copy!

In my room I have two
pictures hanging over my bed.
One is of you and the other
one is of Lou Gehrig. I love the Yankees!
My parents have taken me to
Columbus Clippers games. That's the
closest I've gotten to the Yankees,
but my mom and dad said they
would take me to Yankee Stadioum
some time. I plan to even get married
there!!!! This summar I'm playing
on a softball team called the Saints.
I play Pitchar 3/4 Catcher. So far,
I lead the team in put-outs.

I hope you feel better soon!
Keep your chin up!
Sincerly, Karen A. Lombardo
P.S. I Love You!!!!!!

Mickey Mantle,

Just to type your mame runs chills through my body and I
pray that you'll understand that this isn't your normal fan
letter.

I am 44 years old now, but I'll never forget what I felt as
a young boy in Virginia and what you'll never understand what you
did for me back then. My father was a very abusive man and my
step-mother was an alcoholic(as I turned out to be). As a child,
I needed someone to look to, somebody to be my hero, somebody
to give me strength to make it through another day in my abusive
home. My father would beat me and I'd go to my room and take
out your baseball cards and stare at them for hours as the tears
fell down my cheeks. I held on to my hero, I held on to my dreams
and I held tightly to my young hopes for a better life.

I was always depressed and somewhat suisidal as a young man
and I really needed something to reach out to. Mr. Mantle, you
made me smile, you made me cheer and you gave me a star shining
in my heart that I believe today was the only thing that kept me
going.

I want you to know that my daughters wear #7 on their softball jerseys because Daddy asked them to. It's just a small way that
I can thank you.

I am sad, Mickey Mantle. At 44 years old, I'm sheading tears
in concern for your health. My heart aches knowing you are suffering and I wish I could help you like you unknowingly helped
me.

For that young boy I used to be and for the youngster who
still feels things inside me, I had to write this letter. You will
never know the impact you had on my life and still do. You don't
know how many times you helped that young boy forget his own pain.
You'll never know that boy's gratitude to you and you'll never
know that in reality Mr. Mantle, <u>you saved my life.</u> You gave me
reasons to hope when I was covered with bruises.

Hopefully, you'll get this letter because it means everything
to me right now to be able to express the feelings I couldn't say
as a young boy. Thank you.

Thank you for being Mickey Mantle and thank you
for being a big part of my life, even though you
did not know it.....
Maybe you can know it now.

All my love, my hope, my best wishes, my prayers
and my heart and soul I send to you.

Your dearest friend

Scott Michaels

June 8, 1995

Mr. Mickey Mantle
Baylor University Medical Center
Dallas, Texas

Dear Mickey,

Sorry to hear you are ill. I am writing this letter not to ask you for anything other than to get well soon. I am writing this letter to say thank you; thank you for the memories. I grew up in the 1950's. You were always my favorite player in spite of the fact that I grew up in Houston, not New York. Except for a few games on TV I have never saw you play. But, as many other kids knew back then, you were the greatest...there was no comparison. When we bought baseball cards we would look through them for "Mickey." If we didn't find one we chewed the gum and threw the cards away...there was no substitute. Unfortunately, none of us ever found your card. I guess we didn't chew enough gum!

When I played Little League, we were issued a jersey, leggings and a cap only. Our moms made baseball pants by cutting off an old pair of blue jeans just below the knees and hemming in elastic. I was very proud when we found a real pair of flannel pin stripes at Oshman's. "The Yankees wear pin stripes!!!" I told myself "and Mickey is a Yankee."

Mickey, I have a feeling that God isn't finished with you yet. I feel that He has a purpose for keeping you around for a while. Though the road to recovery will be rough, I feel that it will lead you to great things.

Get well soon...we all love you.

Yours truly,

Harold M. Pharr

Mickey,

I wrote the enclosed piece about one year ago for a speech I was to make. I was 7 years old in 1961 but remember it as if it were yesterday. You always inspired me with your quiet determination — and although you seemed mythical on the ballfield, you were genuinely human off it. Along with thousands of other fans, I am praying for your speedy recovery so that you may go out

and talk to our youth about the ups and downs of being human.

You're still an American Hero. God bless you #7!

Best Wishes,

Howard Rubien

Buffalo, New York
September 1961

The voice came through loud and clear and the boy was amazed at how close it seemed. Outside, the night air was restless and cold. But inside, tucked into brown and white covers on a twin bed that would accompany him through high school, he was as warm as he needed to be.

The voice spoke through the dark night. "This is an incredible story, ladies and gentleman. We are witnessing baseball history as Mickey Mantle and Roger Maris, the M&M Boys, chase the immortal Ruth and his record 60 homeruns. They said the record would never be broken and, yet, here are two young men who may both do it in the same year while playing for the same team. My oh my! Don't touch that dial! The fireworks are just beginning!"

The boy lay there dreaming with his eyes closed and his concsience wide awake. In 1961 the world was before him and the spirit of innocence burned ever so brightly. To know that world was through the crystalized sounds of AM Radio on a cool, fall night in Buffalo, New York. And through the soothing voices of the legendary Mel Allen and Red Barber, he came to fantasize about baseball heroes--men of mythic proportions who's feats were marked by daily box scores and who's nights were spent in faraway cities under bright lights, performing larger than life heroics for thousands of adoring fans.

The boy would go through innings together...the players, managers, fans, announcers and him. The games swirled round in his head and he often pictured himself there at the stadium, under the bright lights, on the bench with the team. The boy was seven and had been to a couple of minor league games at old War Memorial Stadium and they were thrilling. But he could only imagine what it would be like to be at a real major league game! To see the stars and heroes of his youth.

Could I be like them one day, he wondered? I want to be like them, to be their teammate. Perhaps they'll still be playing when I get to the big leagues. We'll all do heroic things together and eat ice cream after the game. People everywhere will love me. Yes, that's what will happen. And, once again, as he had so many previous nights, the little boy's thoughts went dark and in the morning when he awoke the radio was turned off.

\#\#\#

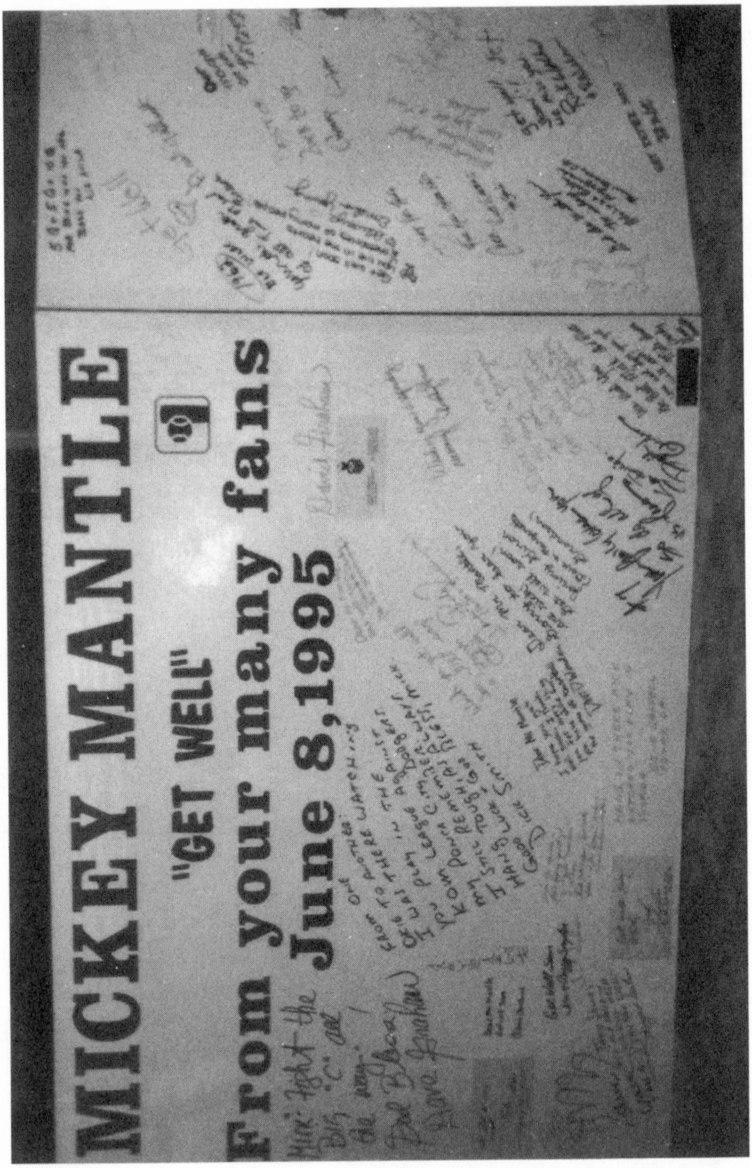
MICKEY MANTLE
"GET WELL"
From your many fans
June 8, 1995

Tuesday, June 13, 1995,

Dear Mr. Mantle,
How are you doing sir?
I hope you get well very
soon. I am sorry about what
happened to you. You are
one of my favorite Baseball
players. My Step-Brother
Stuart Simon who is from
Albany, New York says hello
and he hopes you are feeling
better.

Your fans,
David Shaw
&
Stuart Simon.

Dear Mr. Mantle,

My thoughts and prayers are with you and your family concerning the challenge for life you are faced with. God has a great purpose for your life — even greater than all you did for baseball!

Mr. Mantle, I grew up knowing you were one of the greatest baseball heros of all times. Beyond that, there wasn't anything that I knew of your personal life or problems.

Several years ago, I caught your interview on a talk show, and began to realize the greatness of the Micky Mantle that everyone has raved about for years. Then again on June 7, 1995, they did a re-run of your interview with Bob Costas in which you stated, "I feel I have let everyone down, I feel there's something not fulfilled in my life."

Through those two interviews, I was able to witness an even greater hero and role model that I had envisioned Mickey Mantle being. Today's heros are always placed on a pedestal. Heros are flawless, without heartache and suffering. Or at least, this is how the heros are portrayed. What better hero or role model can we benefit and learn from than by you — with your experiences, heartaches, and suffering? The public will evaporate every word because of the person you are, and the person that has meant so much in our lives.

Mr. Mantle, I hope you will not mind me sharing a personal experience with you. My dad was a hero. He was my very own hero. I believed he was capable to accomplish anything in life.

52

He was kind and gentle to everyone.
His talents and creativity were endless.
But, he failed to recognize his true
potentials. In the interview with Bob
Costas, it was as though I saw my dad
in your eyes and speech.

My dad was a humble man, just as
you portrayed in the interview. He never
gave himself the credits he so richly
deserved. He was his own worst critic!
Your demeanor projected my dad's same
traits! How I wish I could tell
him just how wonderful, how talented,
and especially how valuable he was
in my life. I wasn't allowed the
opportunity to tell him these things
before his death. On September 29, 1981
he committed suicide.

Although I wasn't given the chance
to tell my dad, I don't want to miss
the opportunity to tell you how important
you are in my life and the lives of
millions of others. You're a wonderful
man, a great role model, and a man
with endless talents. God handpicked
you for a special purpose in life, and
allowed you to experience your challenges
and heartaches for good reason. I am
grateful and happy to know you will
be here on this earth with us many, many
more years.

Sincerely,

Anna Seigler

MICKEY MANTEL,

Wishing you a speedy recovery and many more years of <u>healthy</u> living.

As a long time fan of yours since my childhood, as a person to whom I looked up to in my youth, I wanted to let you know that I wish you a speedy recovery.

From the 1950's into the 1960's you were a Spartan god of the baseball world and along with the other classic heros of my youth, Willy Mays, Duke Snider, Roy Rogers, Gene Autry, Billy Grahm, and Bob Hope, and yes even Yogi, you seemed to have left a lasting memory in my mind. Today we seem to lack the positive roll models of the past. Maybe they are still there but are destroyed by a sometimes over zealous press in this era of instant news coverage and ratings wars. Personally I preferred the 1950's and 1960's.

I've outgrown my idol worshipping of those decades past but I still have the memories that you and others imprinted on my mind as a youth. Memories that tended to give me direction and goals at an age when they were needed. Memories that directed my life and channeled my energies in a positive direction.

For the memories you and the other idols of my youth gave me

   I THANK YOU,

     FOREVER A FAN,

      Buster Hummel

JAN 30 1994

Dear Mickey:

I can't remember my last voluntary sober day. Maybe 25 or 30 years ago. I've been to rehab clinics several times, but couldn't find a reason to quit. I lost my family, friends, everything. Just kept on drinking.

You were and are a hero to so many people, me included. I'm 47 years old so I watched you through all the good years with the yanks.

The Babe, the clipper, the mick, then there was supposed to be me. But a line drive between the eyes KO'ed me, never could face the ball again.

I read you were checking in to the Betty Ford Clinic, once again a hero. It takes courage and prayer.

I'm not going to check into a clinic, but if you're going to quit, so am I.

Good luck to both of us. Maybe one day we can get together and throw down a glass of milk.

I love you mick

Manley Davidson

P.S. It's super bowl sunday. It will be strange watching without a beer in my hand. but maybe this time I'll remember who won

55

Dear Mr. Mantle:

This is a letter that I've thought about writing for years, but I never knew where to send it and, frankly, I just kept putting it off until a better time. Well, the better time is now.

First off, I want to let you know that you have been in my prayers. I'm so relieved to hear that the liver transplant went well and that you're on the road to recovery.

Second, I want to thank you for something you gave to me. I was born in New York but moved to Arizona when I was eight years old. My father was a dyed-in-the-wool Yankees' fan. When he was a young man, he even played semi-pro baseball. His greatest joy was watching or listening to a ball game, usually with two different games on at the same time.

When I was a young girl, I didn't, at first, pay much attention to his weekend rituals. By the time I was about ten, I started curling up next to him on the couch and asking questions about the game on television. It was then that I started to notice the husky, blonde slugger from Oklahoma with the big, wide grin. I was impressed with his playing ability and his personality. My daily routine became to check the sports page every morning to see how the Yankees did the day before and especially how Mickey did. It became a link between Dad and me.

He had three older sons, yet it was his daughter with whom he would sit and talk to about baseball. And talk he would. He had a fantastic memory for events, games, and statistics. In addition, he would paint pictures with stories about Ruth, Gehrig, Dimaggio, Dean, Robinson, and others. He made baseball come alive for me, and I gave him an audience to educate and entertain with his favorite subject.

Several times through the years, we made special trips to California to see the Angels play, but always when the "Yanks" were in town. In junior high I'm sure I was an oddity. When other young ladies were reading love stories and chasing boys, I was reading biographies about Mickey Mantle, Willie Mays, Babe Ruth, Yogi Berra, and Roger Maris or just playing softball.

When I was fifteen, my grandmother died, and we made a trip back to New York. One night at the visitation, My Dad walked around whispering to several family members. After a while, he grabbed my arm and said "Come on" and ushered me out a side door without an explanation as to where we were going. Thirty minutes later, about ten of us pulled into the parking lot at Yankee Stadium. My heart raced as I was finally going to see a game at Yankee Stadium. Not only did the Yankees win, but you hit a home run to right center field. It was something we talked about for years.

The Yankees, but especially you, became a link, a strong tie between us that opened other doors. We discussed your accomplishments, failures, abilities, injuries, and, finally, your retirement. About that time, I met a young man, married and had sons of my own, but my Dad and I remained close.

Unfortunately, life pitched us a bad curve, and he died before he could retire and "really" enjoy baseball. In 1972 when I was only 23, he left us; but he left me with many happy memories that evolved from baseball and the "Mick."

It's been said that your life is a success if as you travel your road that you make life better for someone else. I know that right now you may have some doubts about how successful your life has been. Well, I know my life was better for having you cross my path, and I'm sure I'm only one of thousands. Mickey, thank you for the wonderful memories you gave me both on the ballfield and in my personal life.

My heart aches right now for a "special friend" who is very sick, and I pray your recovery is both quick and complete. Be good to yourself and your family, and enjoy to the fullest the innings left in this fantastic game of life.

I hope that you personally get to read this letter as it is a sincere thank you from one friend to another.

God's Blessings,

Dear Mick,

My entire family is pulling for you just as we have in the past both on and off the field. You are as great a person as you were a player! I will never forget being at the Stadium on Mickey Mantle Day when you retired both my brothers and I cried. Nor will we forget that Memorial Day when you went 5 for 5 in the double header with home runs to both left + right field we cried then too! Hang in there - we all wish you the very best. Billy Martin is going to have to wait - we need you here!

Best Regards

Kirs Scully

June 8, 1995

Mr. Mickey Mantle
Baylor University Medical Center
3500 Gaston Ave.
Dallas, Texas 75246

Dear Mickey:

You have been down in the count before when
the big one was on the line. Remember you
are "my hero" so hang in there!

God Bless.

Sincerely,

Eugene A. Cernan

Dear Mr. Mantle,

I watched your presentation on television yesterday. Who says your heart has never been used? You have a huge heart. May it beat forever!

You were great to go on television to tell us about your liver transplant. That took a lot of heart! When you first came up to the Yankees, I was in junior high school. Mel Allen used to tell us on the radio — "Be patient with Mantle — he's just a kid from a small town in Oklahoma." Well, we were patient — and you had a lot of heart to overcome some pretty large obstacles.

Sure you're in our prayers. You were in our lives every day of the baseball year for 18 years. That is a long time to play baseball and a long time to make us loyal, happy Yankee fans.

Thanks for saying what you said about drinking, drugs, school and listening to parents. Your heart was saying a lot to the kids of today.

I wish you health. I wish you and your family many, many, many years of being together so that you may enjoy life. Don't lose your great sense of humor!!

I wish you great success in your efforts to get organ donations. I wish you a speedy recovery so you can get back to playing golf. I wish you can one day return to Yankee Stadium for "Old-Timer's Day" so you can hear all of us cheering again for you and your Yankee buddies!!! We love you guys!

All the best —

Mannie Fontana

CNN

LARRY KING

Dear Mickey

HANG TOUGH.

We Love You Mickey.

Best Always

Larry

Dear Mr. Mantle,

I am fourteen years old - you are my hero and always have been. I was so worried when I heard you needed a liver transplant. I prayed they would find you one. I am glad they found one so quickly and that they are saying such good things about how well you are getting better. I know how scary it is in the hospital - I was in Akron's Children's Hospital just last month. I was scared, but my mom slept in my room so I was not alone. I hope your family is staying with you. I hope this card will let you know that you are not alone ... there are lots of your fans who are thinking and praying for you. I am only one of them. I listen to the news everyday to hear how you are doing - get better soon -

Your friend - Scott

Dear Mickey,

New coverage of your medical challenge has reached everyone. Currently, I'm on "industrial injury" from American Airlines Tulsa Ticket Counter. For six years I've been a ticket agent. Al Jerkens wife, Sandy, was my room-mate in Training. Al is Channel 2 "KJRH Sports" man-of-the-year. We share Mickey Mantle stories. My favorite occurred when I was a Braniff International flight attendant in the 1980's.

You were seated in 4B enroute from Miami to Dallas. I was "oblivious" to your identity. You were "the cute guy in 4B". Anyway - you were enjoying a Tonic of sort. I was enjoying Serving First Class passengers' cold cuts off the serving cart.

The galley girl brought a tray of fresh cold cuts as we were approaching your row. She asked that I transfer remaining items from the cart's tray to the fresh tray. I did immediately —

The airplane hit turbulence and slipped to the captain's right. Three pieces of Italian salami flew out of the tongs and down the aisle — midair — You released your grip on your tonik, caught the "fly-salami", and quietly placed it on the second shelf of the cart.

Shocked I gratefully looked at you. Then Quipped "Hey! you're a pretty good catch!!" You should be in baseball's Hall of Fame." You couldn't believe me and replied, "Others have told me that too, thank you." You returned to your beverage.

In the galley, a man leaned in and said "Jackie, that's Mickey Mantle in 4B". I leaned out, embarrassed, you winked.

Upon exiting the aircraft, you planted a kiss on me I'll never forget.

Your autographed picture hangs in my home. It is still fun to share the memories. God speed a healthy recovery.

Sincerely,
Jackie Christian

63

Dear Mickey,

I am writing this on June 7th, it was June 8th, 1969, I sat in Yankee Stadium, watching you retire. It is a day I will never forget. I was ten years old. Now I'm 37 years old and still feel and remember everything that happened that day.

You are and always will be my hero. I felt compelled to write this card to you. Its kind of like a son writing to his dad just to let him know what he means to him. You are a special part of my life, it's hard to describe, you are a part of my heart. I just wanted to thank you. I'm a Yankee fan because of you, the home runs, the way you ran the bases. Again, thank you Mickey, Good luck.

Jim Barber

June 24, 1995

Dear Mickey,

I know you have received a ton of mail, so I will make
this short. I think you will like the message.

My daughter is a District Judge in Massachusette, with plenty
to say about a lot of things. The very first sentence she
ever put together was----"Mickey Mantle, hit that ball". She
was two years old at the time.

We both wish you a speedy and complete recovery.

Kindest regards,

John J. Deale

Dear Mr. Mantle,

I hope you get well soon. I hope your new Liver helps you lead a long, happy life.

Here is my lucky four-leaf clover. It has been lucky for me, I hope it will help you.

I hope you are feeling better soon!

Sincerely,

Tony Hickman

Dear Mick,

Hoping you have a speedy recovery. You've probably heard this thousands of times, but you are my all time favorite athlete, of any sport. Having written 100's of poems, and having been published, I wanted to put my "gift" into writing, on your behalf. I'm hoping you receive my card - thanks for years + years of inspiration ....

Love,
Bobby Brown

TO MICKEY MANTLE

I'll always love the New York Yankees
And the many memories of my youth
Gehrig, Keller, Joe DiMaggio
Henrick, Yogi, and "The Babe", Babe Ruth

"Scooter", Whitey, and Tommy Tresh
"Reggie, Reggie", he took us higher
Maris, Murcer, and Thurman Munson
Pepitone, and Stottlemyre

Kubek, Willie, and big "Moose" Skowron
Guidry, Gossage, and Righetti
Elston Howard and Hank Bauer
And with the "Catfish" always ready

And through the years, so many heroes
So many champions, there'd surely be
Most every fall, another pennant
Yes, it was, a dynasty

And one player stood out surely
As I followed his career
For he was a young boy's idol
MICKEY MANTLE, every year

That mighty swing, that incredible power
As American as, apple pie
Gracefully roaming in centerfield
Your fame would soar, like eagles, high

For you had the strength of an ox
And God, you ran just like a deer
And oh, the length of your home runs
"Number 7", we held you near

And through the years you had that charisma
As you played with life and zest
A nation's eyes, they turned to you
"The Mighty Mick", you were the best

You hit .300, you knocked in runs
With those homers, out of sight
Some would travel, 5oo feet
From the left, or from the right

And then the inevitable, when you retired
An entire nation could only sigh
A twelve year old, lay down his glove
In '68, he'd cry and cry

For you were a living legend
You were the one who'd "steal the show"
Carrying on that great tradition
After the retirement of Jolton Joe

And to this day, you're still my hero
Looking back now, it's easy to see
The favorite athlete, of a twelve year old
And that boy, of course is me

Dear Mick,   6/7/95

   Although not sure whether you'll actually
receive this, I feel compelled to write none-
theless.

   Your illness has caused me to reflect on my
life, especially my youth, of which you were such
an integral part. Your illness saddens me & causes
me to do something I've never done before, write a
fan letter.

   Please know that my thoughts and wishes for
your eventual recovery predominate & and as I'm sure
you're aware, I'm just one of countless well wishers
moved by your life.

   I'm 41, with two sons, the eldest named
"Mickey." I'm a former college football player, having
also had a ~~to~~ "cup of coffee" with the S.F 49ers.

   In every sport I've ever ~~phyd~~ played, including
"40 + over" softball, I wore/wear No. 7. It was
No. 7 on my vanity license plate, & 7 in the
lottery, etc.

   From 1960-1968, I kept a scrapbook of every
newspaper & magazine article about you. You were the
man, my man, the Mick.

I went to Mickey Mantle Day @ the ~~Stad~~
Stadium with my Dad. I swear you waved at
me when ~~you~~ you rode by in the cart.
How I cried.

When the N.Y. crowd was tough on ~~you~~ you,
I was incensed. Certainly aware that you were
human both on the field & off, your courage
in light of your ~~injury~~ injuries, your flair for
the dramatic HR, the youness of you, transcended
all.

Mick, you cannot underestimate or downplay the
profound effect you have had on me and
many like me. Although a somewhat street-wise
kid from New Jersey, the magic of your aura,
was overwhelming.

For better or worse, you are An American
Hero. A larger than life icon, to whom I
can point to my sons & say "You can be
Anything you want to be."

You take care of yourself Mick.

You will Always be, My Hero, My Idol.
Sincerest regards for your recovery,

Michael P. Terrizzi

June 8, 1995

Dear Mr. Mantle,

I have been wanting to write this letter for a long time and I feel that this is the proper time to do so. I am 45 years old and have been a fan of yours since I first knew what playing baseball was all about and I continue to be a loyal fan to this day. To put it simply, you have been my idol and always will be. My lifetime dream has been to meet you personally and shake your hand and I still hang on to that dream.

With all the talk over the years of the drinking and partying with Whitey Ford, Billy Martin, I guess my denial of your ever having a problem with alcoholism was strong. After all, you were my idol. As a youngster, I proudly wore #7 on any baseball uniform I could, that is if other kids didn't beat me to it (my son who is 13 plays on a Babe Ruth team that I coach, The Grand Forks Yankees, and wears #7).

When I read the article that you had in Sports Illustrated regarding your alcoholism, I cried, not because my hero was alcoholic, but because of your acceptance of your illness and not being afraid to publicly voice it. I to am an alcoholic/addict and needed to enter treatment to address my addiction. That was thirteen years ago and I proudly can say that I am clean and sober today. I am also an addiction counselor at United Hospital in Grand Forks, North Dakota and see the devastation that addiction brings everyday. I know that some patients read that article while they were in treatment and related to what you were going through, as did I. Even though I never met you, I felt closer to you and understanding your life through what you shared. After all, that is the premise of AA and I applaud you for your sharing.

I am deeply saddened by your current health situation and am scared for your life. I hope and pray that you can come out of the hospital following your transplant and continue to live a strong, healthy and productive life. You have given so much to me over the years that if there were anything that I could do to help, I surely would. My thoughts and prayers are with you and your family during these difficult times. Someday I do believe that we will meet and I will hold on to that boyhood dream forever.

Gods blessings from a fellow AA member and a fan forever,

Bob

Bob Alvestad
Grand Forks, North Dakota
(75 miles from Roger Maris' hometown)

August 1, 1995

Mr. Mickey Mantle
Dallas, Texas

Dear Mickey,

My radio crackled me awake at six am this morning and the first news story was about you. Not a good way to begin a day.

I know you have legions of fans and I, also, am a great fan of yours. I was born in 1951, and I believe that it was your rookie year. I cannot imagine what my childhood would have been like without you or Roger. When the time came to distribute the Little League uniforms, the numbers 7 and 9 were actually fought over.

I remember that I used to get fighting mad when you batted left. I wanted you to bat right because I batted right. But that was before the days I realized that baseball also contains strategy. You just don't always step up to bat and fit into the grand scheme of things.

Some of my best childhood memories involve watching the Yankees on Sunday afternoon with my dad, and listening to Ol' Diz and Pee Wee call the game. *Them wuz the days!* as Diz might say.

All my best to you, my lifelong friend. (Please forgive my familiarity but I have known of you all of my 43 years.) You and your family are in my prayers and thoughts. You will ever know all of the young lives you affected in a positive way and we all are pulling for you.

Sincerely,

Phil Sartin, Jr.

Dear Mr. Mantle,

God's Blessings and continued private & public prayers for you, dear friend. I am a priest alone in an inner city parish of 1300 families.

I first saw you play at Fenway in your great years of 56 or 57. You launched a line drive torpedo off the steel beam above the left field wall; and the umpire missed it — making you stop at 2nd base!! The Yankee fans, especially me, could not believe the bad, bad call. Casey #37 screamed for 10 minutes & was sent to the showers.

I met you personally at an East Providence Super Super Market Opening a few years ago. You signed a "K55 Mantle" bat for me that still sits here in my office. We spoke for two or three minutes about your good son Bill, who has gone to heaven recently.

You must be getting 100 letters per day, so I better sign off for now. Keep swinging, Thanks for your wonderful work for transplants and charity donations, and your good leadership. One Thing is very sure — God Loves You; & prayers in old Providence, RI will be constant.

The Best — "The Mick" from a lifetime fan & 55 yr. old pastor —
Fr Jim Farley

74

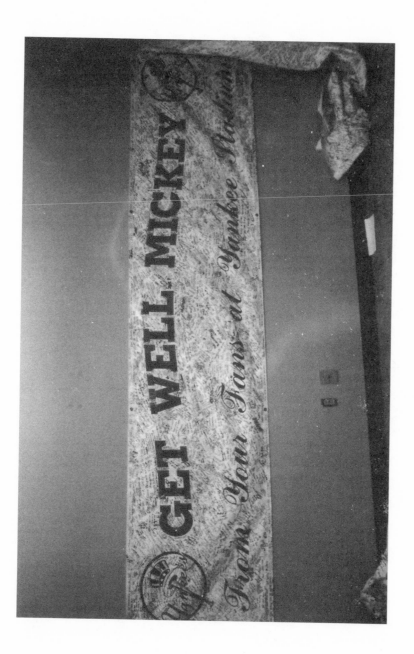

June 8th, 1995

Mr. Mickey Mantle
Baylor Hospital
3500 Gaston
Dallas, Texas 75264

Dear Mickey:

As soon as I heard about your illness, I wanted to write to assure you of my prayers, as well as those of all my family.

Although we haven't met you personally, we have been admiring you since the beginning of your career. As a youngster I went to Yankee Stadium to see you play, later when I got married, my husband and I went to see you (I wouldn't have married him if he weren't a Yankee fan) and when our son was born, it was natural we would name him Mickey, in your honor. Well, our Mickey is now 29 years old and has three children of his own....and all our family still follows the Yankees - no matter what.

But even above being a Yankee fan, we always recognized and admired your greatness, as a professional but even more as a human being. Considering all you went through during your career, you still persisted and that makes you **THE GREATEST**!!!!!!! We firmly believe that had you not been injured at the very beginning of your playing years, **NOBODY** would have even come close to you as a baseball player.

Now it is time for us to give you something back for all _you_ did for all of us and since we can't do much, we would like to assure you of our love and prayers for your quick and complete recovery.

We know God will bless you and your family and that He will allow you to live for many more years.

With much affection and great admiration,

Mary

Dear Mr. Mantle,
   I heard about your liver
transplant. I had a liver transplant
too. I had it on January 19, 1995.
I had a few complications at **first** and
had to have 2 more operations, but
now I feel great.

   I'm 10 years old so I was **too**
young to ever watch you play baseball,
but I know you were a great player.
The 1 thing I love more than fishing
is baseball. I am well enough to
play baseball in a kid-pitch leauge.
I am pitcher on a team called the
A's.

   I just wanted to write you a
letter to wish you well. I am including
a baseball card of myself from this
year as a reminder that you will get
well.

                    Sincerely,
                 Patrick K. Flavin

DEAR MICKEY:

MY MOM & DAD WERE DIVORCED WHEN I WAS VERY YOUNG AND I HAD NO REAL
FATHER FIGURE IN MY LIFE. I WAS SMALL, FLAT-FOOTED AND SLOW, NOT
AT ALL GOOD IN SPORTS - MY MOM WOULDN'T LET ME PLAY ORGANIZED BALL
BECAUSE OF MY SIZE. THERE WERE FEW OTHER BOYS IN THE NEIGHBORHOOD
SO I SPENT MOST OF THE TIME BY MYSELF. I THREW THE FOOTBALL TO
MYSELF AND I BOUNCED THE BASEBALL OFF THE HOUSE TO PLAY CATCH.

WHEN I WAS EIGHT (1962) I DEVELOPED MY SPORTS ALLEGIANCES FOR THE
TEAMS ON TOP AT THE TIME (PACKERS, YANKEES, & CELTICS) - I HAVE
KEPT THOSE FAVORITES OVER THE YEARS AS WELL. BUT I GREW UP ADMIRING
RUSSELL, STARR, AND YOU, MR MANTLE. BASEBALL WAS MY FAVORITE SPORT
AND YOU WERE MY FAVORITE ATHLETE. EVEN THOUGH YOU NEVER KNEW IT,
YOU SHAPED MY LIFE DRAMATICALLY. I LEARNED THREE THINGS FROM YOU
THAT I AM VERY PROUD OF TODAY: TO PERFORM UNDER PRESSURE & IN THE
CLUTCH, TO PLAY (PERFORM) EVEN WHEN YOUR INJURIES (OBSTACLES) ARE
GREAT, AND MOST IMPORTANTLY, AND SOMETHING LACKING TODAY, TO WIN
OR LOSE WITH GRACE & DIGNITY. NO OTHER MAN IN MY CHILDHOOD SHOWED
ME THESE THINGS AS YOU DID.

WHATEVER THE OUTCOME OF YOUR FIGHT WITH CANCER WILL BE, I AM SURE
YOU WILL AGAIN PERFORM WITH GRACE & DIGNITY. MY PRAYERS HAVE BEEN
AND WILL BE WITH YOU. THANK YOU SO MUCH FOR WHAT YOU HAVE MEANT TO
ME THROUGH THE YEARS.

SINCERELY,

LOUIS GALLAHER

Mr. Mickey Mantle
Four M Limited
8080 N. Central
Suite 800
Dallas, Texas 75206

Dear Mickey,

In your continuing battle with cancer, we wish you only the best. Enclosed is a resolution unanimously enacted on June 15 by the New York City Council wishing you well. The thoughts and prayers of New Yorkers are with you.

Sincerely,

Kenneth K. Fisher

THE COUNCIL

June 14, 1995

Res. No. 1044

Resolution wishing Baseball Great Mickey Mantle a full return to health and a quick recovery.

By Council Members Fisher, the Speaker (Council Member Vallone), Council Members Ognibene, Freed, Malave-Dilan, Eristoff, Eisland and Fusco; also Council Members Koslowitz, Leffler, Marshall, Michels, Robinson, Williams and Abel

Whereas, Mickey Mantle is one of the greatest players of the Golden Age of New York Baseball, who hit 536 home runs in his baseball career and helped to lead the New York Yankees to play in twelve World Series; and

Whereas, Mickey Mantle has recently encountered even more difficult challenges than those he faced during his 18 seasons as a Yankee; and

Whereas, Mickey Mantle is confronting serious health problems with same level of courage that helped him to win seven World Series for the City of New York; and

Whereas, This baseball hero of the 1950's and 1960's is now in Baylor University Medical Center in Dallas, Texas recovering from a liver transplant and receiving treatment for Hepatitis C which he contracted from a blood transfusion; and

Whereas, The talent and effort of Number Seven in centerfield and at home plate is a continuing source of inspiration for all New Yorkers; and

Whereas, Even New York Mets fans know that Mickey Mantle, nicknamed the Commerce Comet, is one of the greatest baseball players and the hero of generations of Americans; and

Whereas, The grace and power of Mickey Mantle and other great baseball players brought generations of New Yorkers together and gave divergent groups a common cause; and

Whereas, New Yorkers pray for Mickey Mantle's return to the same level of energy that powered a home run 565 feet in April of 1953; now, therefore, be it

Resolved, That the Council of the City of New York wishes Baseball Great Mickey Mantle a full return to health and a quick recovery.

Adopted.

Dear Mickey—

I am 54 years old. In 1956 I was 16 and you and the Yankees had had a great year. My mother and step-father were living in New York and were at the Stadium for Larsen's perfect game. I was at boarding school near Toronto, and I loved the Yankees, especially you.

That December my parents came up from New York and we had Christmas dinner with my grandparents. As was his custom on this occasion, grandfather put a verse he had written about each person around the table and we had to find the verse that described us to know where we were supposed to sit.

There was no verse for me, Mickey. I had no place at the table.

Grandfather began a lengthy apology when suddenly the doorbell rang. Moments later my younger brother entered the room with a telegram addressed to me.

Everyone was watching as I opened the yellow envelope. Inside was a message: "Merry Christmas, Frank, from your friend Mickey Mantle."

Grandfather had pulled another of his famous coups, this time on me, and I was his very willing and delighted victim. I had my seat at the table after all, and a season's greeting from my only baseball hero.

I have never forgotten that event, manufactured as it was just for me, and the thrill I felt to think that you would actually send me such a thoughtful note. Time passes, Mickey, but memories remain to warm our hearts and remind us of the joy of innocence and the power of belief.

Life isn't easy, as you and I know, but there's still time to right wrongs and heal pain. I have an 8-year old son named Patrick. I don't know if he can have heroes the way I could have heroes.

We love you, Mickey, those of us who listened to your games on the radio, who held our breaths when you and the others came to bat, who lived and died with every swing you took.

You were our champion, Mickey, and you still are.

So hang in there, and know that we're thinking about you and praying for you.
                                Frank Stephenson

Dear Mickey,

I remember cheerin' you on when I was a kid. God, you were my hero. That was "over" 30 years ago. Where'd the time go?

I want you to know I'm still cheerin' for you, and wish you success with your operation and with your health.

Along with the cheering, I also threw in a few prayers for good luck. I feel it's like going to the "big Bullpen in the sky" for relief. Ha! Ha!

Take care & get well soon!
xxx
Mike Goss

P.S. You'll always be "Mickey Mantle" to me!

Dear Mic,

On the 23rd of May 1959 for my seventh Birthday I got a Mickey Mantle Signature Baseball Glove which I slept with that night.

You were my hero even before that. I followed your career and still get excited even to day when I here you name, because it brings back those fond memeories of growing up a Mickey Mantle Fan.

My hopes and prayers are with you as you go through these troubled times. But I Know in my heart you will get better cause I still want one day to shake your hand.

Love & God Bless
from one number 7 to another.

Don

Dear Mickey,

I most sincerely wish you a speedy recovery.

This past summer at Old Timer's weekend I had the great opportunity of meeting you personally in your restaurant - an experience I will never forget.

You see Mick, I grew up watching every move you made - everything was baseball to us kids and you were IT! I admire you to this day. So to have met you personally means a great deal to me. I'm still behind you.

Mickey, let me offer these few kind words to my boyhood hero: As you well know we all have crises in our lives.

I can fully understand your present dilema. But you can get through this one .... just believe in yourself and take it one day at a time. Know also that there are lots of people out there pulling for you all the way - we continue to believe in and have faith in your success. Just keep going.

In the meantime, I believe in Mickey Mantle.

Soon I'll scrape the money together and fulfill my next dream — to own one of your Upper Deck signed baseball bats!

Mick, if there is anything I can do for you in some small way, please feel free to call on me at any time.

Best wishes from me to you, Mr. Mantle..... win, lose or draw, you're a New York Yankee, aren't you?

Sincerely,
Tim Linden

June 7, 1995

Mick —

Hang in there big guy,
it's only the bottom of the
sixth. We need you for the
rest of the game.

Glenview Baptist Church

A
FELLOWSHIP
OF PRAISE

Dear Mr. and Mrs. Mantle:

How we are praying for you, thankful for the progress you have made this week. Mr. Mantle, you have always been one of my heroes. As a boy, I used a Mickey Mantle glove, bat and wore your number 7 on all my uniforms. One problem - I never could get the ball over the fence!

You're still my hero, Mick. Now that my daughters have graduated, I look forward to telling my grandsons about you. As I speak to young people in schools all over the world, one of the things I notice lacking is a hero in their lives. I was fortunate; I had - and have - so many heroes like yourself.

I know you've been through a lot of pain, physically and in so many other ways. I have a tape of your television interview when you expressed your problem with alcohol, how you wish you could do things over, especially with your boys. I don't think you ever stood taller in my eyes, and I know your family was so proud of you. Thank you for being man enough to admit failure and willingness to begin again.

That's exactly what I'm praying this will be for you both: a chance to start over. Of all the things God has done for me, I think I appreciate the fact that He is a God of a second (and third, and fourth....) chance, willing to help us as we trust Him. I know you realize what a miracle He has worked on your behalf, in answer to your prayers and the millions of us who have prayed for you. And we will keep praying that you will grow ever stronger.

You and my Dad are about the same age. How he loved you! One of the last things he was aware of was the autographed baseball of Mickey Mantle that I took to him. He recently passed away, leaving hundreds of people loving and admiring him. I hope you know that there are those of us who feel the same way about you! I know that I speak for your wife and sons when I say we want you around for a long, long time.

I asked some of our Tuesday luncheon guests to sign the enclosed card. It comes with the thoughts and prayers of our entire church. We just didn't have room for 4,000 members to sign it, but know we in Ft. Worth will continue to lift you, Mr. and Mrs. Mantle, and your family to our Lord. Know, too, that you've got a Baptist preacher pulling for you, and if you ever need a pastoral visit, I would be honored to stop by on my rounds there and talk baseball.

Sincerely,

Dennis Baw, Sr. Pastor
and the Congregation of Glenview Baptist Church

8-9-95

DEAR MICK,

Hope This Finds you improving.
Thanks Mick For a million memories.
You were The greatest Baseball
Player ever.
There was no greater sight
in all of sports Than of
you legging out a bunt
when everyone expected another
Towering home Run. And
watching you make catches
in The Field That other players
only dream of.
Remember Mick, There is
a Field of dreams somewhere
in Iowa. Someday maby I
will have The privlidge of
pitching Batting practice To you.

All my Best Mick.
Get Better Soon.

VELDON LAUDER

Dear Mr. Mantle:

I want you to know how very happy I am that you have survived your ordeal of liver failure and transplant surgery.

Although we have never met, you have been an inspiration to me at two distinctly different periods in my life. I suspect that you have had the same impact on others, and I would like to thank you.

When I was a child, I admired you as the greatest baseball player that I had ever seen play. This admiration was pure and uncritical, as a child's admiration tends to be. You did not really inspire me, because I was a polio victim with no illusions at all about being able to match your skills; but I admired you wholeheartedly and was entertained by you for many, many hours.

Some time around high school I lost interest in baseball, and I never watched another baseball game, although I always remembered you fondly when I heard your name. A child's heroworship was over, and no other athlete that I admired as a child has had any subsequent impact on my life.

Recently, as an adult successful by the standards of outside ovservers, I have come to admire Mickey Mantle in a completely different way, and in fact be inspired by him in a way that I never was as a child. When I heard that my childhood hero had a serious drinking problem I was not only sad, but I could relate to that. As a person, I certainly have on occasion had feet of clay.

Then the real miracle of Mickey Mantle arose. If Mickey Mantle could finally rise up and whip a severe drinking problem (and apparently a genetically linked one at that), I had one extra piece of inspiration for dealing with my own human problems. Mickey Mantle could not inspire me as a child to be a great baseball player; but he was able to inspire me as an adult to deal with my human problems, no matter how serious.

For that adult inspiration, I can never thank you enough.

Get well soon, and God bless you.

Sincerely yours,

C. Keith Powell

C. Keith Powell

Dear Mr. Mantle

My name is Derek Rau. Last September I had a Liver Transplant too. I was eight years old when I had mine. Now I am nine. It has ben nine months since I had my transplant. If you need to know anything you can call me at 1-810-786-1912 but don't worry you will be up and around before you know it. I had to go back to the hospital over 4 times. My doctor is Peter Whitington. before my Transplant I was rushed to four different hospitals in two days. None of them knew what was wrong or could help me ___ ... until I got to the University of Chicago in wyler's childrens hospital. My Dad was supposed to give me part of his Liver but then he didn't have to because we got a donor. Since January, I have gone back to school, played roller Hockey and baseball and I am feeling very good. My mom told me that people who have had transplants are very special, like you and me. I am sending you a picture of me after my transplant

Sincerely,
Derek Rau

MICKEY MANTLE
BAYLOR MEDICAL CENTER
DALLAS, TEXAS 75246

DEAR MICKEY,
                        I'm SURE THOUSANDS
OF LETTERS ARE being sent To you EVERY
DAY, SO you probaly will never see This one,
I'm Just A Jewish Guy FROM BROOKLYN, who's been
A YANKEE FAN FOR 52 YEARS, I'm nobody IMPORTANT
JUST A Mickey mantle FAN FROM DAyone. Although
you ARE Just Three years OLDER Than me, You
ARE my Idol Always have been, Always will
be, I Saw Them All, but you will Always be
ONE To me. AS I sit here writing This
Letter I AM crying + praying FOR you.
My wife happens To be Italian And she is
Lighting CANDLES FOR you in CHURCH. MAY
G-D Be Good To you, MAY G-D WATCH over
you, And MICKEY Thanks FoR The Memories.

                LONG TIME YANKEE FAN
                Irwin Beck

Mickey Mantle
Baylor University Medical Center
3500 Gaston
Dallas TX 75246

Dear Mickey,

I was sorry to hear that you had to return to the hospital for cancer treatment. I originally thought I'd send flowers but I decided that a short letter would be more meaningful. I also suspect that your room is full of plants and flowers.

I wanted to tell you how much you meant to me as I was growing up in the 1950's. At the time I lived in Hawaii and was crippled with severe club feet. As with million of other youngsters, you were my hero. I wanted more than anything else to be able to play baseball like you. My dad was well aware of this and managed to get a ball autographed by you and the rest of the '55-'56 Yankee team as you traveled through Honolulu to Japan for an exhibition game. My dad gave me that ball after I emerged from corrective surgery at Tripler Army Hospital and told me that if I worked hard at it, I could play ball like my hero Mickey Mantle did.

I was determined to do just that. Once my casts were removed (3 months) and I went into braces I started working on running, hitting and catching several hours a day in spite of how weird I may have looked to others. I spent a lot of time swimming also. After a year, the fruits of my efforts finally were born. I was able to play little league ball with the rest of the guys. After two years, I even made the All Star Team (no more braces). I had to play first base or pitcher because I was not fast enough for the other positions. Throughout this entire time, I followed your career in wonderment. To this day, I am convinced that you were one of the main reason I was able to gain the use of my feet and go on to a normal life.

I thought you might like to know how much you inspired a young 8 year old so may years ago. By the way, I still have that ball.

My prayers are with you for a full recovery and a resumption of your new found life.

Sincerely,

George S. Eckhardt

Dear Mr. Mantle:

I am a 10 year old girl who is a big fan of yours. I had a Liver Transplant 1 year ago because I had cirrosis caused by a virus And I am doing wonderful. I know what you are going through but don't be scared. You will feel like a new person. ALWAYS drink your medicines on time and follow the doctors orders.

I pray for you to have a quick recovery. If you need help in any way please let me know.
A slammer is what you play Pogs with and I have one of you.

Your #1 fan and friend
T.J. ♡

My nickname is T.J.

June 12, 1995

Mickey Mantle
C/O Baylor University Hospital
Dallas, Texas

Dear Mickey,

I am a forty-seven year old Mickey Mantle fan. I last wrote to you when I was ten or eleven years old, and I still hold you in the same esteem now as I did in 1958. The last time I wrote to you I asked for an autographed photo. This time all I want is for you to get well.

I have an eleven year old son, Mark, that obviously never saw you play, but he sure knows who Mickey Mantle is. He is learning the game and doing very well. When we play together I still remember all those times I was Mickey Mantle stepping up to the plate. Now he is doing it also. I'm not sure who should be most flattered, you or me. In any event, I want you to know my prayers are with you. You were always the best, my hero, and you still are.

Sincerely,

Ed Leach (signed Eddie in 1958)

August 02, 1995

Mickey Mantle
% Baylor University Medical Center
Waco, Texas

Dear Mick,

Since 1956, I've followed the events of your life, and harbor the utmost respect for your great talents and achievements, including the treat of having seen you blast number 534 (on a 1-2 count?) Your baseball career was a boy's dream to follow. And I'm glad to have been a boy during the days of Mantle, Maris, Mays, Aaron, and the other great *Boys of Summer*.

Yet, at no time was my respect for you greater than last year, when you sat alone on a stool, fielding questions from Bob Costas. My feelings for you were so great that I shed tears for both of us, and for all others who've experienced the heartache of drug use.

At this time, there aren't words easy to say, or easy to hear. There are some, however, I'd like to hear. Please find a camera, with great exposure, Mick, and say,

"Drugs kill, boys and girls! Please don't use them! Please don't use *any* of them!"

I think you can affect a whole other generation with your honesty, charm and presence. What a legacy. I love you, Mick.

Sincerely,

Michael Fox-Lambert

Because you are
   still my hero.
You gave me a love of
   baseball.
Now you give me an image
   of courage.
      Teresa Schuxabe

Dear Mr. Mantle,

I felt compelled to express my sadness & grief at learning of your illness. I've never written to anyone under these circumstances. I'm 44 yrs-old and on or about July 03 '61, my father took me to my very first ball game. Needless to say, I wanted to see the Yanks win. I think the visitors were the "KC Athletics" and by or about the 3-4 inning, the Yanks were down 7-1. As far as I'm concerned, this was the greatest baseball game because not only did the Yanks come from behind but they went on to win 8-7 and if I'm not mistaken you hit that deciding homer in the bottom of the 9th which was typical for the great clutch-player that you were. You may also recall that it was this game in which both you + Maris hit back to back home runs twice! think if you will, the elation I felt at the age of 10 to attend a game of this magnitude.

I pray you'll have the opportunity to 'send one more over the fence' and recover this illness. I pray you don't suffer and you're granted more years.

Needless to say, Ali was good but you were the 'greatest'. Your name transcended the sport - come from behind, Mick, again, and show 'em that you don't give up so easy!

All my very best wishes for a speedy
    + healthy recovery:

    Jack Amont

PS: I've become so disinterested in base-ball, I don't even watch it anymore. You were more than a player; you were an idol. You gave too much joy to too many people to be considered just a ballplayer.

Dear Mickey:

As a fan of yours almost since I was born, I want you to know how much you are in my thoughts and prayers during this difficult time. I hope and pray that you will have the strength and good fortune to get through the next few weeks, and that you will soon be out of the hospital and back on the golf course.

I can't tell you how much a part of my childhood you were. I still drag out the home movies my mother took of my sister and me standing at the fence with you in St. Petersburg during Spring Training in 1956 (I was 5), and show my kids the best ballplayer who ever lived. Night after night I would listen to the Yankees on the radio, resting up for another day of playing baseball, where we would fight over who would play center, or who would be you in Home Run Derby. Saturdays were always reserved for the Game of the Week, with Dizzy Dean. I'm sure the Yankees weren't on every Saturday, but it seemed like they were. October was even more special, racing home from school to watch you and the Yankees win yet another World Series.

Watched excerpts from your interview with Bob Costas last night. I think you wouldn't be human if you didn't have a few regrets for the way you lived your life. I think we all have regrets, things we should have done differently, or better. The important thing is that we learn and go on, and not focus on all the dumb things we did in our past. Like most of your fans, we can forgive you a few mistakes, because of all the joy you gave us on the field.

Again, Mickey, I'll be praying for you and a speedy recovery. God Bless You!!

Sincerely,

John Zorn
Grapevine

BILL "FIREBALL" BEVERLY

"MICK"
YOU HAVE ROUNDED
3 Rd. NOW HOOK
SLIDE INTO HOME
"SAFE"
IT Will BE OK
Bill Beverly

STAMP

AMERICAN NEGRO LEAGUE LEGEND

June 9, 1995

Mick,

Hope you don't mind me calling you that, but as a fan who hung on your ever at-bat, I almost feel as if you're a personal friend.

In fact, when I was a kid of 7 or 8, I would listen to the Yanks on the radio and, if you were having a bad day, I just knew it was because I was listening. And every time I'd turn it off so you'd do better, you did. If you were 0 for 2, you'd end up 3 for 5, or something like that. At least it seemed that way to an idolizing kid.

I can't turn that radio off this time, but I still know you're gonna be doing a whole lot better by the time this gets to you. Hang in there Mick, we're all pulling for ya.

A fan forever,

Russ Havourd

Columbia University in the City of New York

DEPARTMENT OF ENGLISH
AND COMPARATIVE LITERATURE

Philosophy Hall
New York N.Y. 10027

June 7, 1995

Dear Mickey Mantle,

I write as an old loyal fan, wishing you well. As a boy in Washington, D.C., you were my greatest hero. I went to the ballpark, old Griffith Stadium, never to see the local bums, the Senators, but to watch you play, to study your moves — as runner, as fielder, and especially as hitter. As a Little Leaguer, I tried my best to capture your stance and the quick explosion and stride: and the sweep of your magnificent swing. It was — that swing — and is the stuff that dreams are made of.

Let me add that I was a black boy growing up in a segregated city. So for survival's sake, I knew what race meant, somewhat. But race had nothing to do with idolizing you — except perhaps that I felt if I could just be half as superb a ballplayer as Mick, then no race barriers could ever stop me.

I never became a ballplayer, not since high school. I hung up that ambition to go to college, and then to pursue a career as a college professor and writer. But I want you to know that what I got from you has helped me in these latter careers as well. For me you were the exemplar of what it meant to be a pro — stylish and cool at the top of the game; never giving up; tough; beautiful These same qualities come through in your book as well.

During this season of distress, please know that you have many fans who wish you all the best and who pray for you. I am one.

Best Robert O'Meally

Professor of English

13 July 1995

Mr. Mickey Mantle
Dallas, Texas

Dear Mr. Mantle,

I'm sorry I didn't write sooner. Considering the extravagant importance you held in my childhood, I received the news of your illness with surprising equanimity. My dearest friend died recently, so perhaps there were no tears left over. Still, after reading about your press conference, I felt impelled to write.

You were quoted as saying: "I just want to start giving back. All I've done is take. Have fun and take." This simply isn't so. Intentions are awfully hard to pin down, and sometimes our reasons for doing things are obscure even to us, but whether your inspiring heroics as a youthful athlete and a symbol of triumph over physical adversity would have been even more astounding if you had taken better care of yourself cannot be known. Your "having fun" was important to us. Fact is, for many years you've made many people very, very happy. Who's to say who deserves love? Over the course of those years you won ours.

As for "giving" and "taking": don't forget, we also "took" from you. Some of the expectations you felt pressure to fulfill may have come from within you or your family, but they also were thrust upon you by us. We can't judge you—most of us haven't felt comparable pressures. And you should not judge yourself too harshly. In your own way, you've been "giving" to us—people whom you don't even know—for most of your life.

I hope you become physically strong again and live healthily for many years. But I also hope that you feel some peace in the knowledge that what to you felt like "taking" and just "having fun," meant "giving" us memories we shall cherish throughout our lives.

Be Well,

Dennis

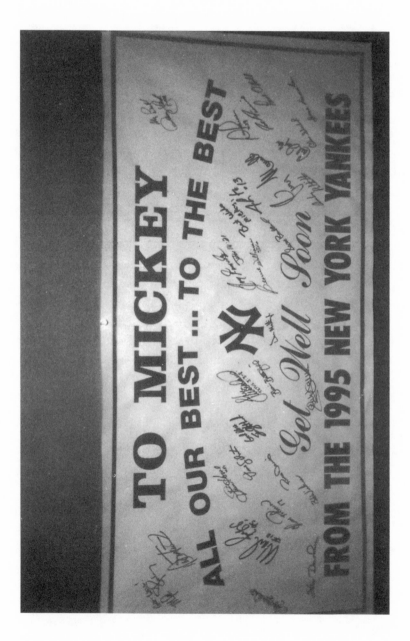

August 11, 1995

To my all-time favorite hitter--

I can't let you sit in that hospital without my taking the time to at least write you a note. I never write fan letters-- the only two I've ever written have been to John Wooden and to James Michener, but this is an exception.

I've been a fan forever. I was a junior high and high school student in a little farm town in Wyoming when your career was at it's peak. The Yankee games were broadcast on a station with high enough power than even a little town like that could pick it up. You were my hero from then on.

After I married and moved to California I made my husband take me to Angel Stadium when you played there. I took the only picture of a baseball player I've ever taken (it's such a tiny slide that you're probably unidentifiable, but I know who it is!).

I just wanted you to know that many of us are out here thinking of you and wishing you every good wish for a speedy recovery.

Much love,

Carolyn Nukaya

Mick —

I haven't cried or prayed so hard since my dad passed last summer. I know yours was equally special to you.

You also are special to me, first as a childhood hero, and now as an inspiration to curb my own abuse of "adult beverages." I pray each day that you make a complete recovery!

God Bless you - I can't wait for the day I can shake your hand to say "Thanks!"

— Larry Winslagel

2/17/94

Dear Mickey:

I certainly hope you receive this letter and read it, for you should know that there are many who are in your position, Mickey, maybe not as famous, but have endured the pain and have had the courage to take the first step. Many, including myself, are proud of you and that is a ~~fact~~.

I grew up in the Pittsburg Ks, Joplin Mo. area in the 50's and 60's and always wanted to meet you. Well, I did meet you at a card show in Denver last summer. I was taken by how tired you looked at that show and I'm glad you've had the courage to seek treatment. Its a cliche, but the steps you have taken is actually the beginning of the rest of your life, which will be a long one I'm sure.

In my office in one of my rooms I have a "famous persons' wall decorated mainly for my child patients. 90% of the items are pictures signed by you for me, magazines, articles etc. I've been amazed at the number of children ages 6-12 who know who you are and are wide eyed when they see your signature or read an article about you and your colleagues from the "golden days of baseball". I spend _many_ more hours discussing all these items with the kids than adults. These memories are never dead while they remain alive in the minds of these kids. I don't mean this to be an emotional discourse or a "pat you on the back" type letter Mickey, but I do want it to help you realize the many adults and kids who are proud of you

I had an adult the other day come in and make the statement, "Well now what do you think of your hero, Dr Bettus". My reply was that I probably have more respect and admiration for you now than I ever did before. He just shook his head and said, "Well you've got to give him credit". . . . (Probably an old Dodger fan, right.)

I do hope I'll have the chance to see you & speak to you sometime. All the best to you _and_ your family.

Warmest regards
Raymond S. (Ray) Bettus

February 8, 1994

Dearest Mickey,

We are writing to reach out and let you know how much we love and care about you. We just wanted you to know that we're routing for you Mick.

My wife + I grew up worlds apart, she in rural Georgia and me in Queens County, New York. We both agree on how much of a true hero and a great man you are. You were a hero and someone to look up to back in the pin stripe days and, more than ever, you still are. The luster that was Big No. 7, back in the baseball days, has never tarnished or faded - instead it has only grown brighter as the years have past. We love and admire you for who you

really are - not as the greatest baseball player of all time (although in our minds and hearts you truly are), but as a warm and beautiful person who forever touched our lives with your own unique style and grace, humility, compassion and feeling for others. It is your humanity that sets you apart, in a league by yourself. You are as good as they come, and we are so very proud of you.

For so many years on the diamond you showed us all great courage in working through adversity and pain. Now, all these years later you are again showing us the same courage and fortitude - this time

not in a game but in a real life struggle.
As always, Mick, we know you're going
to come out the winner that you are.
Our hearts, thoughts and prayers are
with you.

Just in passing, Mick, I want
to let you know how much an honor
it was to meet you back in the
Summer of 1965 in the Yankee dressing
room. I was there with my dad as
guests of Cletis Boyer, as arranged
by Commodore Stone of Tulsa, Oklahoma.
Thank you for being so gracious and
warm to a 16 year old boy. It
meant alot then, and it still does.
Thanks Mick - I've not forgot and
never will.

God bless you Mickey. We truly
love you and wish you all the
best - that is exactly what you
deserve.

Tom + Pat Grace

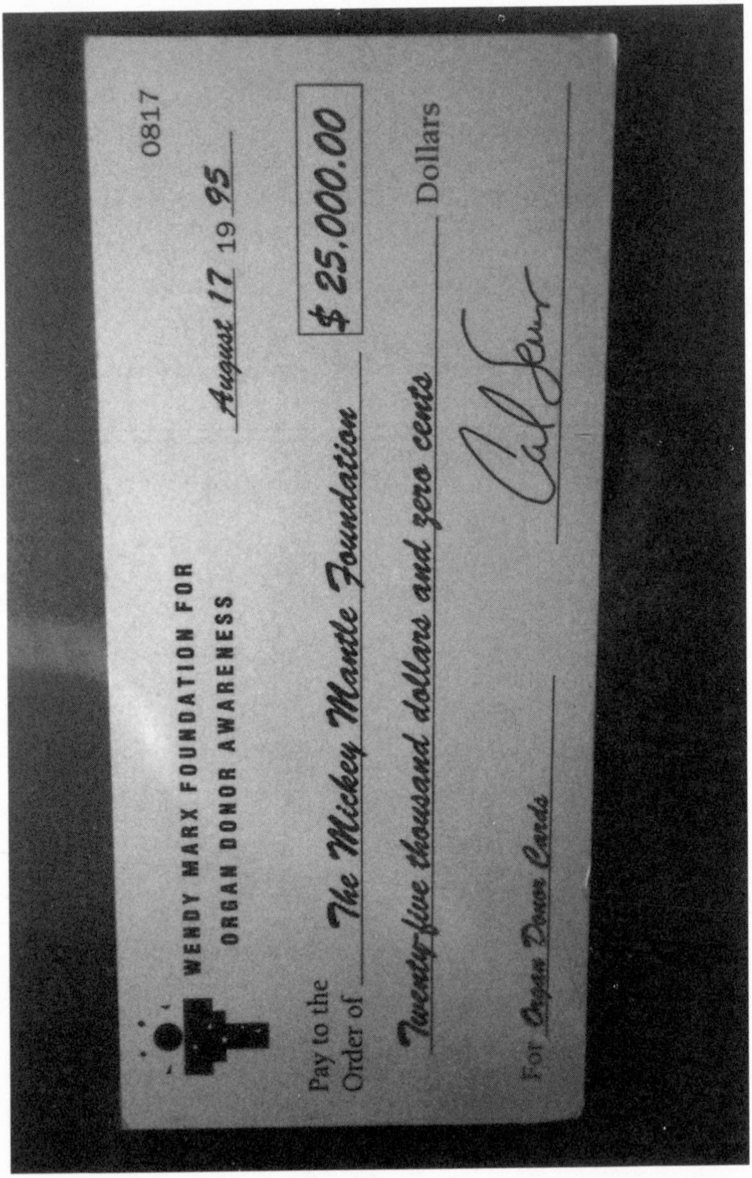
WENDY MARX FOUNDATION FOR
ORGAN DONOR AWARENESS
0817
August 17 19 95
Pay to the Order of The Mickey Mantle Foundation
$ 25,000.00
Twenty-five thousand dollars and zero cents
Dollars
For Organ Donor Cards

Dear Mick,   6/7/95

I know that these few words
will be but a drop in the deluge of
best wishes that you will receive over
the next several days, but none me
more heartfelt.

When I was 12 years old my parents
divorced and I had to move to Texas with
my mother. I lost my friends, my
hometown, my teams, my school —
but I did not lose you and the
1960 Yankees. Via my transistor
radio And the newspaper I stayed with
you; you were my anchor when all else seemed
remote and fading.

I've been lucky to meet you and
shake your hand on two occasions
since then. Your photographs and
autograph look down on my desk
as I write this.

Thinking of you always
reminds me of the best parts
of my childhood. You were
important to me then, you're
important to me now.

With all my best wishes
for a full and rapid recovery,

Harry Alexander

6/15/95

Dear Mick

I don't watch Baseball much anymore. The Spark, suspense, and I
guess the Magic is missing. Oh,
There are still great players, but
they all look + play alike.

I have seen and heard you on
TV lately, and you really seem
down on yourself, primarily, you
say for not accomplishing more in
your Career. Well, you know
what inside you, but I know how
I felt each time I saw you play
"Goose bumps". I really didn't care
if you hit the ball or not, I just
wanted to see Mickey Mantle.

You gave people a thrill just by
being on the field, running or limping,
hitting or missing, we didn't care.
You may not have been the Greatest
in the game, but you were the
greatest for the game.

We are the same age, you and I, and both old ball players, (not in the same league of course), but I always thought you were much younger, for you did everything with such grace and power.

Your up to bat again Mickey, this time with a new liver and a new Chance. Take it.

Don't be so hard on yourself. The booze and the bad times are gone. Remember, we love you because you enhanced the game you played such a short time — More than anyone else.

Who else do you know that could have taken Joe "D"'s place. My thoughts and prayers will always be with you and I thank God I live in a time when a Kid from Oklahoma could become the greatest Yankee of them all.

Warmest Regards

Eddie H Sprogg

Dear Mickey,
                    I have been a
Baseball coach for 24 years now
and have gone through what
you are about to go through.
              As you know it might
be the toughest game that you are
yet to play - But it can be
won.   I admire you for
taking that 1ST step towards
1ST Base and as you round
all the bases and head for
home you will become a
better player and person the
next time you sit in the dug-out.
              You have always been
my favorite player and now
truly not only mine but a
lot of others inspiration.
              Youre the Best'
sincerely,   your Pal & fan always Mike

January 30, 1994

Mickey Mantle, #7
Betty Ford Center
Rancho Mirage, California

Dear Mick,

I read in the paper that you have checked into the Betty Ford Clinic. I am presently 42 years old and have been following you for many years. I am a fifth grade teacher in West Hartford, Connecticut and have just finished a unit on Drugs and alcohol with my kiddoes. I read the article on you and immediately thought of my kids. We discussed your entering the clinic. The children were particularly adamant that what you are doing is important first of all to you and second of all to people everywhere as a model of identifying a problem and doing something about it.

In any event,, Mick, we're all thinking on you. I'm willing to bet that Billy Martin is smiling down on you wishing you his best , too.

Hang in there.

Sincerely,

Doug Cramphin

June 10, 1995

Dear Mickey,

I have been a fan of yours all my life.
My Dad is a die-hard Yankee booster and I
guess its rubbed off on me in a big way.
I remember when I was 14 years old listening
to the Yanks play our hometown Angels. You
hit a grand slam and I was overjoyed. But
when the Angels came from behind to win
I was so disappointed for you I punched
a hole in my closet door and needed 14
stitches to sew up my arm. When I told
my Dad what I'd done, and why, he
wasn't even mad. He understood.

Now I've got 4 kids of my own and
they know alot about you and your career.
My family is keeping you and your family
in our prayers, and I send you our very best
wishes for a speedy and complete recovery.

You have been an inspiration to me and
a source of memorable times that my Dad
and I have shared together watching and
listening to you play.

Thanks for the memories and get well soon

God Bless You,

Mike Miller

118

Dear, Mick the Stick, you are so sweet you will always be in my

dreams Love your Baseball Hall of fame Person, Brooke D, ROWE

x hugs
o kisses
XO XO XO XO XO XO

June 9, 1995

Dear "Mick":

As the entire sports world focuses on its concern for Mickey Mantle, one guy in particular is praying for your speedy recovery — A 46-year-old State trooper from Winder, Georgia. A guy whose father taught him to read the newspaper box scores when he was only six years old so that he could find out if Mickey got his hit today. If there were "goose eggs" in Mickey's column, the young boy would have a bad day. If there was an HR in that column, or maybe two HRs, then it was like Christmas — All day.

Now that boy is middle aged and can't bring himself to remove his display of Mickey Mantle items from the corner of his study. It seems the older I become, the prouder of these objects I become. I speak of commemorative plates, miniature statues, cards, rare photos, etc. Yes, sir, these bits of nostalgia will always have a permanent place in my home wherever my home shall be.

I have always admired the way you carried that broad Oklahoma frame around the base paths after blasting those BB shots into the upper seats. Recently during a televised interview

With Bob Costas, you told us why you buried that chin so deeply into your chest when you trotted around the bases: "So not to show up the opposing pitcher." I think that statement tells the entire Mickey Mantle story— a man blessed with an amazing ability to play baseball (the best who ever walked onto a major-league diamond), but a man who was also blessed with the ability to handle his talents with humility for himself, and with respect for the other guy.

A few years ago I was assigned to the Georgia State Patrol Security Division at the Governor's Mansion in Atlanta. I had the opportunity to see you a couple of times while you were visiting Governor Miller, another devout Mantle fan; but unfortunately, I didn't get to meet you. I did, however, watch you talking with the governor for about 15 minutes as I peered from the security office. Yes, that middle-aged six-year-old boy was having his dream come true—a real-life view of "the Mick."

Mickey, you're the baby boomers' last living hero, and I'm sure everything is going to work out fine, and you're going to be better than ever. We just won't have it any other way. God bless you, Mick.

Sincerely,

Dennis Huff

7 June 1995

Dear Mickey

This letter is about 27 years overdue. . .but let me regress just a little.

When I was growing up, you were the man I loved the most in baseball. When you and Maris were in your home run hitting duel, I cried when he went ahead of you. I can remember that day distinctly. I was about 12 or 13.

When the Yankees were in the World Series with the Dodgers in 1963, my family flew from Denver to LA to see two games. You tied Babe Ruth's world series home run record that day at 15. This came after I'd seen you board the bus to go to the stadium, and cried for 20 minutes because it was so exciting to see you.

The man I married when I was 19 was also a fan of yours, and two weeks after we found out I was pregnant, my husband suggested the name "Mickey" for a boy. We never wavered for an instant, and in May, 1968 my Mickey was born. We were living in the Dallas area at the time, and I kept meaning to take Mick to see you, but it didn't work out. He could pick you out of a team picture by the time he was two, though, and has always had an affinity with you.

We've been to "your" restaurant in New York City several times and continue to be great admirers of yours. You are a legend and a nice man. I am so glad you have been such a special part of my life, even though you never knew it. You've made a difference in the lives of many people. Bless you!!!

I wish you the very best now. I pray for your highest and best good to come to you and I KNOW you will be taken care of.

With a special kind of love

Judy Owens

February 2, 1994

Mr. Mickey Mantle
c/o Betty Ford Center
Rancho Mirage, California

Dear Mr. Mantle:

I am a 32 year old Yankee fan who, like millions of others, idolizes the man who wore number 7. I read about your attempt to overcome alcoholism by entering the Betty Ford Center. I am convinced that anyone who has accomplished what you have in your lifetime could also attain your latest goal -- an alcohol-free life. Imagine, if you will, that all your fans are cheering you during this "turn at bat" and alcohol is the pitcher trying to strike you out. It's the bottom of the ninth and the score is tied. As you have done before, you pass Elston Howard who is waiting on the on-deck circle. Please tell him to go back into the dugout because you will hit the ball so hard and so far it will never come back again.

Very truly yours,

Philippe D. Katz, Fan

June 25, 1995

Dear Mickey,

I always called you Mickey. I know some fans called you The Mick. You were big and strong when I was little. I saw you hit a lot of home runs and make a lot of hard catches. I memorized your numbers. Your averages and steals and RBIs. I'd run downstairs in summer to read the box scores to see how you did. I saw them carry you off the field in Baltimore. Your name was on my glove and all my life when I see or hear the number 7 I think of you. I suffered growing up. And as a man. You helped and didn't know. I'm sure a million kids, some not too young anymore, feel the same way I do. You can help us again. One more time. Live.

Bob Butcher

June 27, 1995

Mickey Mantle
Baylor University Medical Center
3500 Faston Avenue
Dallas, TX 75246

Dear Mr. Mantle,

I have never rooted for you as much as I am rooting for you now.

I wish I could do more than that. I wish I could help. I wish I could tell you how much you have meant to me my entire life. When I was a kid, growing up in Iowa, you were my hero—next to my dad—just as you were to a generation of kids who grew up in the middle of nowhere who dared dream of greatness.

I wasn't very athletic as a kid, but everytime I took a grounder to the chest, I'd think of you and your dad, and I'd work that much harder. I've tried to instill that in my two sons and my daughter. They will thank you someday.

When I was 12, Dad took me up to Minneapolis in 1965 to see you and the Yanks. Before the game, I looked up, and there you were, ten feet away. Dad told me to ask for your autograph. You'll probably laugh, but I was simply too awestruck to move. Just being in your presence was enough. (You walked, Tresh homered, and the Yanks won, 2-1. Heaven!)

When I heard about your illness, I broke down and sobbed. It was unlike anything that has happened to me as an adult. Just like when I was twelve, your presence has been enough. The thought of you leaving us so soon was just about unbearable. Forgive me for blathering on so, but I don't know any other way to tell you what you have meant to us.

God bless you, Mick! You and your family—and those doctors and nurses who saved you—are in my prayers.

Sincerely,

Wayne Spies

Hi Mickey,

You don't know me, but I have been a fan of yours since I was a young child.

I will never forget all of the joy and excitement you "ol' yankees" gave me.

Dam, you guys were great.

I hope this works for you. I know how alcohol can "take" ones life.

I've been there before.

Take care Mick & God Bless

A Fan!
Bob Herzog

June 7, 1995

MR. MANTLE,

My prayers are with you to get well soon! My name is Joe Alford and I play Bass Guitar with country artist Collin Raye.

In the mid-1960's when I played little league baseball, <u>you</u> were my hero. You were a great role model and gave me interest and inspiration in sports. This kept me healthy and out of trouble. I just wanted to say thanks and let you know that when I was a kid you touched me and made a difference in my life.

Once again, my prayers are with you and may God bless you.

Sincerely,

Joe Alford

10 August 1995

Dear Mickey,

I am writing to thank you for the times you have unwittingly helped me over the years. As a tomboy growing up in New York in the '60s, one of my big thrills was following the Yankees. My dad had always been a big Yankee fan, and now it was my turn. Mickey Mantle, of course, was our favorite player.

My dad and I didn't have much in common at the time, but I could always count on you to give us something to talk about. Our usual conversation began with, "What did the Yankees do today? How did Mantle play?" One particular memory etched in my brain is swimming in a friend's pool and my dad coming over to let me know that "Mickey just hit another one." Thanks for helping me share these joys with my dad.

I went on to name my first pet turtle Mickey, and I did a book report on The Quality of Courage. My dad took my sister and me to the stadium for Mickey Mantle Day — we wouldn't have missed that. Later, I named my good luck charm Mickey — it was a little plastic troll with blonde hair and a green body. With Mickey close by, I passed big exams and completed grueling marathons.

Now 41 years old and a wife and mom, I'm still one of your biggest fans — although now it's for the courage you've shown of late. When you played for the Yankees and were hurting, I used to wish that each of your thousands of fans could share a little of your pain. There were so many of us that none of us would have felt anything. I have the same wish today.

Thanks for all the memories you've given me, Mick. I can't wait to tell my one-year-old son all about you. I pray for you nightly.

with appreciation,
Donna Elliott

June 27,1995

Mr. Mickey Mantle
Baylor University Medical Center
3500 Gaston Avenue
Dallas, TX 75246

Dear Mr. Mantle:

  With all the years that have gone by since I was a boy in Queens listening to the
Yankees on the radio, my family still remembers how I would cry when you struck out. I
remember only how I cheered when you hit homers. Then I would go out and hit one in a
stick ball game in the P.S. 32 school yard -- but very few lefty. I'm still cheering for you,
and hope you get well soon.

Sincerely,

Franklin J. Havlicek

Dear Mickey:

In my 8th grade year book, 1957, I wrote that I one day wanted to play along side of Mickey Mantle for the New York Yankees. You were my idol then and still are today. What ever made me think I could play with the likes of you?. Well I had speed, power and an arm like a howitzer with accuracy liken to a laser sight. My power? At age 15 I hit one of your homers. My high school coach measured it at 476'. Until 3 years ago, when the school closed, there was still a plaque on the fence where the ball left the field. I had that dream of playing next to you and when you were through of being the next Mickey Mantle.

I've heard you say that you felt that you let your fans down. Yes you let many fans down but those were those fair weather ones. You know, the ones who cheered you when you hit a homer and booed when you struck out. Your real fans cheered for the homers and hurt with the strike outs. They hurt because they felt for you. They knew you had given your best and had come up short. If they played any ball they knew what your insides must have felt like. I know I had a lot of those big swings for a third strike and I know how I felt inside. Did you let me down? Never!!! You never will either.

I've heard on the radio how things are and might be with you, but I also know how hard you've fought through the years and I know you're fighting now and as in the past, you'll come through.

Now I'm not a religious man but if it's prayers you need, I'll pray. If it letters, I'll write them. If it just someone to talk to, I'm here and always will be. You were always the man I wanted to model myself after. Like you I had leg problems from high school football, but unlike you, after surgery, I was afraid I'd reinjury the knee and end up crippled and therefore gave up. I've never forgiven myself for that but I've always been proud to say that Mickey Mantle was my idol. A man who always gave his best, even though he probably hurt enough that if it was the average person, that person would be in bed.

Hang in there and continue fighting, your family, friends, fans and the sports world need people like you.

Sincerely, your devoted fan

Garey D. Cearlock

Garey D. Cearlock

June 9, 1995

Dear Mickey — I tried to find an appropriate
         get well card but what do you send to
    your hero?

I'm 47 years old and for several summers of
my youth I was you. I've kept all of the
scrap books and read all of your books. I'm
very happy for you and your family that the
" Commissioner in Heaven" did not draft you
yet.

     It seems as if God has a good enough
team right now and we still need you here.

     Hang in there champ. You have always
shown courage and came thru in the
clutch.

                    Best wishes,
                    Sam Quinn

Baseball is life

FROM: Billy Shoemaker
TO: Mickey M.

August 2, 1995

Dear Mickey,

As I was growing up in Northern New Jersey in the 50's, I was
fortunate enough to have an Uncle who bought tickets to all the
Yankee home night games, and he was kind enough to take me to
most of them with him. What a thrill for a young boy to be able
to witness baseball history being made by the Yankee's, and
especially Mickey Mantle. I remember names like Yogi, Whitey,
Scooter, Roger Maris, Irv Noren, Gil McDougald, Casey Stengel,
Moose Skowren, Andy Carey, and on & on. Thanks for all the fond
memories.

I hope you recover very soon from your current health problems.
The work that you have begun encouraging public awareness of
organ donors may be the best thing you could ever be associated
with. You see, my wife has had a kidney transplant for the past
19 years. It truly saved her life, so I can relate to your
enthusiasm promoting organ doantions.

You brought a young boy many great thrills as I grew up. Hang in
there and God bless you !

Very truly yours,

FRANK YORKE

Dear Mr. Mantle,

The stands are filled tonight with 50 year old kids like me; our hearts are filled with countless memories, gratitude and best wishes for your complete recovery. I'm sure we each have our own special moment. For me it was one warm Bronx evening, sitting behind the Yankee dugout, against Baltimore, I think; batting righty. you hit a grounder to deep short, everyone knew it'd be close at first; you were flying down the line, fans screaming their encouragement and then in a flash, you went down, a few steps short of the bag, a hamstring tear. I remember the vast and utter silence that descended on the stadium and remained even on the subway train going home. I just wanted you to know we're still here, with our memories of your courage and dignity — our thoughts and prayers are with you; our cheers and silence —

Sincerely & greatfully
Mark Kroll

MARK KROLL

Dear Mickey:

I was deeply saddened to hear about your illness.

I started first grade the year you won the Triple Crown, and I suppose that's the year I first became aware of who you were. I have a framed enlargement of your 1956 Topps baseball card hanging in my study. One of the moments I remember most vividly from my early childhood came when I opened a one-cent Topps package and found your 1957 card.

You were everything I wanted to be when I was a kid growing up in Misenheimer, N.C. I was lucky enough to have a little ability as a baseball player, and I learned to switch-hit a little so I could be more like you. I think what I admired most about you was your determination to play despite injuries and pain that would have benched most players.

The main reason I admired you, however, didn't have anything to do with your baseball statistics. Even though you were one of the greatest players to ever put on a major league uniform, you still didn't seem too different from the rest of us.

Now, almost 40 years after I first heard of Mickey Mantle, I know more about the sadness of your life and the mistakes you made. I want you to know that I still admire you, and for the same reasons I did when I was a kid. You're like the rest of us because we all make mistakes and regret some of the things we've done or didn't do.

What separates you from most people, however, is that you're willing to admit your mistakes and regrets, not just to yourself and those who are close to you, but to millions of people. You endure this public pain because you want something good to come from it. Just like you did in your playing days when you played with injuries to help the team, you've put aside your own pain to benefit others, hoping they'll learn from your mistakes. Don't ever think that you aren't a hero and a role model. You're one of the most couragous men alive, and I still want to be like Mickey Mantle.

Sincerely,

Willie Drye

DEAR MICKEY —

I'M A 52-YEAR OLD PHARMACIST FROM NEW JERSEY AND I'VE BEEN CRYING ALL DAY THINKING ABOUT YOU.

YOU'VE BEEN MY BASEBALL HERO SINCE I WAS 12. I LOVE YOU. I'M PRAYING FOR YOU TO GET WELL.

I MEMORIZED YOUR STATS. YOUR 565' HOMERUN. YOUR TRIPLE CROWN. I WROTE ODES TO THE MICK.

GOOD LUCK FOR A QUICK RECOVERY. A LOT OF US MIDDLE-AGED KIDS LOVE YOU.

Jerry A Belber

March 30, 1994

Mr. Mickey Mantle
c/o Betty Ford Center
P.O. Box 1560
Rancho Mirage, CA 92270

Dear Mr. Mantle:

I recently read an article (copy of which I have enclosed) in the <u>Milwaukee Journal</u> Sports Section about your stay at the Betty Ford Center.

You, sir, are a great man - a man who will be forever remembered in the annals of sports history and in the hearts and minds of millions of baseball fans the world over, many too young to have ever seen you play but who have listened to their fathers and grandfathers across this great country as they handed down the legend of Mickey Mantle to the next generation; a great man who had problems just like the rest of us but, unlike most of us who often live in denial, made the choice to face his problem head on with the courage to admit it to himself and then seek help. It takes a great man, a strong man, to do that.

Three and one-half years ago I met a wonderful woman who helped me face my problems and addictions and helped me turn my life around. I now have a successful photography business and a happy life.

Your strength in the face of adversity and the unfortunate passing of your son, Billy, for which you have my deepest sympathy, is an inspiration to people everywhere. You have love and respect from an entire nation because, Mr. Mantle, you are a great man.

Sincerely,

Paul H. Neumann